BURPEE AMERICAN GARDENING SERIES

PERENNIALS

BURPEE

AMERICAN GARDENING SERIES

PERENNIALS

Suzanne Frutig Bales

MACMILLAN GARDENING

U.S.A.

Macmillan Gardening
A Prentice Hall Macmillan Company
15 Columbus Circle
New York, New York, 10023

Library of Congress Cataloging in Publication Data

Bales, Suzanne Frutig.
    The Burpee American gardening series. Perennials / Suzanne Frutig Bales.
        p.   cm.
    ISBN 0-671-86393-2
    1. Perennials.   2. Perennials—Pictorial works.   I. Title.
    II. Title: Perennials.
    SB434.B35   1991
    635.9'32—dc20   90-34511
                                                            CIP

Designed by Patricia Fabricant
Manufactured in the United States of America

9   8   7

First Edition January 1991

PHOTOGRAPHY CREDITS

Agricultural Research Service, USDA
American Daylily & Perennials
Bales, Suzanne Frutig
Billhardt, Elizabeth
Cresson, Charles O.
Dibblee, Steven
Frowine, Steven A.
Horticultural Photography, Corvallis, Oregon
Ray, Frederick (Rick)
Rokach, Allen
Schreiner's Gardens
Still, Steven M.
Viette, Andre

Drawings by Michael Gale
Garden Plans by Richard Gambier

Garden Designers:

Adele S. Mitchel (preceding pages); Alice R. Ireys (pages 6, 16, 23); Bayberry Nursery (page 10); Suzanne F. Bales (pages 11 and 21); Old Westbury Gardens (page 12), Charles Cresson (page 14); J. Barry Ferguson (page 19); Connie Cross (page 22); Marco Polo Stufano at Wave Hill gardens (page 24)

I am happy to finally express my deep gratitude to the many people who have helped me while I was writing this book. My thanks go to Gina Norgard, Martha Kraska and my husband and partner, Carter F. Bales, for providing me with unending help, support and love and to Alice R. Ireys, my close friend and mentor.

I am indebted to horticulturists Chela Kleiber, Eileen Kearney, Steve Frowine, Carol Whitenack, Charles Cresson, Jim Hoge and Ralph Borchard; to the Burpee breeders Dr. Dennis Flaschenreim, Teresa Jacobsen, John J. Mondry, Dr. Nung Che Chen, Dr. Michael Burke and Lois Stringer; to Jonathan Burpee and the Burpee customer service department; and to photography coordinator Barbara Wolverton and administrative assistants Elda Malgieri and Kathleen D'Azanzo.

At Prentice Hall I would like to thank Anne Zeman, publisher, editor and gardener, whose watchful eye, patience, enthusiasm and belief in these books have made them a reality; Rebecca Atwater, whose twist of a phrase and change of a word have greatly improved and polished these books; Rachel Simon for her patience and thoroughness.

Cover: Spiky, blue Perovskia *contrasts in form as well as color with the flat, open flowers and ferny foliage of yellow coreopsis 'Moonbeam' at Filoli Gardens in California.*

Preceding pages: A perennial border, backed by trellises of climbing roses, blooms in July with astilbes, delphiniums, lilies, and phlox. The yellow spires of Eremurus bungei, *a summer-flowering bulb, set off the border.*

CONTENTS

Introduction

Perennials creep up on you. They take you by surprise! Before you know it, the fascination becomes an addiction. There: You've been warned! It is nearly impossible to have only one, or even two or three. My husband's answer, when asked about our ever-expanding gardens, is, "It could be worse. What if she loved diamonds?"

When we moved to our present house twelve years ago, there wasn't a garden on the grounds, just a clump of peonies, a cluster of Japanese irises, and a heavenly fragrant honeysuckle vine draped over the door. The honeysuckle taught me the power of fragrance. All summer long, every time I go in and out the front door I thank the man who planted that vine, and the God who created it. If I have to visit the city, I pick off a flower and put it in my pocket to carry the fragrance and a little of the garden with me. It's the best perfume I know.

From the day we moved in, perennials began to arrive. A bed of ivy quickly established itself, having run over a nearby fence. A friendly bird dropped clematis seed under an evergreen, where it flourished. In early September we have the only blooming evergreen around. Little white flowers, like twinkling Christmas lights, hang in pretty, random patterns. It was probably a different sort of bird who brought us the New England asters that bloom in October under and around our forsythia. Goldenrod just appeared one day, knowing he was safe from false slander (not the culprit of hay fever, as some believe). I have learned to love and admire goldenrod, the golden plume of autumn. I've even moved goldenrod a few times, planting it in front of the deep purple-blue berries of beautybush and behind the New England asters. Not many people can boast of a blue and yellow garden in October.

I divided and replanted the peonies, anxious for as many flowers as possible that first year. The Japanese irises I moved to the edge of the woods where I could see them from the porch. I knew the garden books said "full sun" but I thought this was where I could best admire them and disregarded any advice. They bloomed halfheartedly and put on the dismal display of a sulking child. Why is it that even with all the experts, some of us still need trial and error?

I planted a variety of purchased perennials from the local nursery in the rectangular, island bed where I had dug the peonies and irises. It was a strange location. I could only see a corner of it from the porch where we enjoyed summer meals and lazy afternoons. Somehow it didn't occur to me in those early days that I could move it. Please, learn from my mistakes. Do as I say and not as I have done. Gardening is always an adventure, and with a little help from your friends you will take fewer wrong turns.

Each year—almost without realizing it—we added to our garden. (Gardening, not just perennials, can creep up on you.) When you first start gardening, you worry about maintenance: How do you do it? Maintenance is easier for me today than it was when I first began because now I better understand the needs of perennials and how to care for them, and I have a routine. It's like the difference between having a single child or half a dozen. Perhaps the only child is more scrupulously cared for, always perfectly groomed, but the larger family is usually more easygoing, full of companionship, laughter, and unexpected events. A mother with a larger family has to keep lists, be better organized, step a little quicker, and constantly keep a watchful eye, never expecting all of her children to be well-behaved at the same time. Well, life in the garden is like that. Perhaps having four children has made me a candidate for more gardens.

Gardening is a love that keeps growing. Borrow freely any ideas you find in the pages that follow, and may the joy of gardening carry you happily through the seasons.

The author's blue, pink, and silver border in mid-June. Papaver orientale 'Show Girl' in the front lives up to her name, commanding attention.

THE PERENNIAL GARDEN PLANNER

Perennials are like people. There are the bold and the meek, the quick and the slow, the sloppy and the neat, the thugs and the saints. Some are so charming that we overlook their weaknesses or excesses. Some run rampant and need to be banished entirely, especially from small gardens; other enthusiastic varieties can simply be contained ("good walls make good neighbors"). There are no "bad" perennials, only perennials in the wrong spot. Their environment has a lot to do with their behavior and their beauty.

A perennial is, strictly speaking, any plant that survives more than two winters. The perennials we discuss here, however, are such herbaceous plants as daylilies, chrysanthemums, and peonies, grown for their ornamental flowers and foliage. Even though the stems of perennials (with a few exceptions) die back to ground level each winter, their strong, hardy roots send up new shoots each spring, usually for many, many years. The best results with perennials come only after the second year, when the plants are thoroughly established.

Some short-lived perennials like columbines return for three or four years, often reseeding themselves before they disappear. Long-lived perennials like peonies can outlive most of us with their life expectancy of one hundred years. Some perennials are easy-going; daylilies, for example, seem to tolerate sun, part shade, clay, sand, heat, cold, and any other trials encountered. There are the fussy perennials like *Lobelia cardinalis* that won't tolerate any condition except wet feet, and the difficult delphiniums that demand nothing less than cool, moist summer nights and rich, damp soil are easier grown

as annuals. Both *L. cardinalis* and delphiniums are so spectacular in bloom that gardeners in all the wrong climates constantly experiment to see if they can keep them growing from year to year.

There are perennials in every imaginable color, in a wide range of plant heights, habits, and foliage types. A particular variety will look different and respond differently in different gardens. Some perennials grow well in hot sun, some in shade. Some are excellent for cutting, some are easy to dry for winter bouquets, and some are wonderful for eating. One of the great challenges of gardening is the creation of a perennial border offering many kinds of flowers living in harmony.

Flowering perennials have always been popular with gardeners, but in recent years a new peak of popularity has been reached. Why? Because most perennials are fairly easy to grow. They're a good investment, multiplying themselves every few years with very little help from you. They're versatile, providing gorgeous bloom in succession, spring to fall, everywhere in the country, anywhere in your yard.

We have listed over eighty perennials in this book and have even included a few biennials, the plants that flower their second season and usually reseed themselves. My favorites, foxglove and Canterbury bells, fall into this category. But this is just a beginning. We hope that your curiosity will encourage you to seek out new and different plants. This is an exciting and fulfilling pastime, coaxing their best from perennials through patient care and observation, always remembering the old paradox: Mother Nature is commanded only by being obeyed.

A late June perennial border meandering along the edges of a stream features irises, artemisia, lilies, and astilbes planted with ornamental grasses for a very natural-looking garden.

WORK WITH NATURE

Perennials planted in bold groupings of sunset colors form a meadow garden around a sculpture of a sail-boat. Plants include rudbeckia, achillea, echinops, daylilies, Crocosmia, and ornamental grasses.

In planning any garden, first study your grounds for the best place and shape. A garden conveniently near the house will give the most pleasure to busy people. Designing a perennial garden means learning to work with Nature. Only by living on intimate terms with a garden can its beauty be fully enjoyed in the ever-changing light and atmosphere, and its needs quickly realized and satisfied. House and garden should seem insep-arable, complements to one another.

Planning a garden is one of those big jobs that seems smaller and more manageable when the steps are taken one at a time. Step-by-step planning will not be overwhelming, and it will bring out the artist in you and give you a sense of accomplishment. You'll find that, from the dreams at the start, to the selection of plants, right through watching the garden grow and mature, your garden will bring you great pleasure and pride. Closeness to Nature is its own reward.

Ask yourself what it is you want from a garden. Do you want to be able to view it at a distance from the porch? Will it be a place to stroll, sit, or enjoy meals? A secluded spot to enjoy in private, or one to bring pleasure to all who drive by your home? Look at all of your reasons for having a garden, then try to imagine whatever problems you might need to overcome. Is the chosen site near where the kids play ball or where your dog runs? Is it a low area that becomes soggy after heavy rains? All of your criteria can be met if you plan carefully. Taller plants with bright colors can be used to help your garden show up at a distance. Some resiliant perennials can stand up against the follies of kids and dogs; daylilies, hostas, *Lysimachia*, and Shasta daisies are some of the toughest. Any problem you might encounter has a solution. Rely upon the bounty of Nature, be-cause there are plants for every place and purpose.

When you are clear about your needs and the demands of the garden you contemplate, consider the site. Just as the house comes before the furniture, the site is selected before the plants. Don't choose your perennials first and force them to live in a place that isn't right for them. Every garden picture is improved by a frame: the sea, a wood, a hedge, a wall, a court-yard, a terrace, a hillside, or the house itself. Of course, an actual, four-sided frame isn't needed, but a backdrop, enclosure, or other element will help "anchor" the gardens. Any or several of those mentioned, and other boundaries, natural or artificial, can show a garden's particular beauty to best advantage.

Respect the elevations and depressions of your land and try to work with them rather then immediately assuming all gardens must be flat. You'll save money and achieve a more interesting design. Every plot of land, like every human face, has an individuality to be emphasized rather than overcome.

Set your priorities. The temptation is always to attempt too much. Do one garden well the first year. You can always expand later, and the time you spend planning well first will pay off. Just as it takes time and study to decorate an interior room, it takes time and planning to develop a garden. The more thorough you are, the fewer surprises or disappointments later.

Patterns After Nature

Creating patterns in the landscape to echo patterns in Nature is one way to approach garden design. Plant white astilbes to drift down a hillside, where they will look like waterfall cascades. Day-lilies massed along a property line, swelling and receding, recall a river rambling through the countryside. "Brooks" of primroses can babble boldly with bright color among trees in a shaded area. Waves of low-growing cerastiums and dianthuses can surround and spill from rocks. For a natural look, paths shouldn't be entirely straight, and plants should spill out over the path, softening the edges.

Imagine a meadow of three-foot perennials, one color drifting into the next, or a rainbow garden, a display of color in a rainbow's orderly fashion. These are a few examples of the many ideas you can play with while designing your garden.

GARDEN STYLE

No single garden can fit every site. Really, there are no two gardens alike, which adds to the charm and surprise of enjoying others' gardens. Here are the most basic styles of garden design:

♦ *A garden to walk through, divided by a narrow path that cuts straight, curving, or twisting through it*. The path can be of any length and should be bordered by a width of 3, 4, or 5 feet of perennial plants on either side. It can lead to your doorway, follow a stream, meander through the woods, or wander along the border of a long, narrow property. Shrubs can be planted in the garden for emphasis, to block out an unpleasant view or to direct attention to a fabulous view. Surprises can be planned at every turn: unexpected colors, a beautiful flowering shrub, a garden statue, a birdbath. The walk through the garden can be a walk of discovery. Perhaps the garden walk ends at a pond, an elevated site with a view, or something as simple as a buddleas shrub covered with butterflies.

In old-fashioned gardens of this type, paths curved and turned to bring the stroller back over the same ground only a few feet away from where he had first walked. It was considered poor design for any part of the path to be visible except the one the stroller was on. However, the longer and more twisting the path, the more difficult it is to plan. Lining a relatively short, already existing walk to a front door is a good project for a new gardener. With careful planning, an experienced gardener can lay out a proposed new path with a garden hose, study it for a few days or a week, and then decide. Consider a design that takes shape over the course of several years (especially in the case of more elaborate designs); such gardens are usually very successful and worth the wait. Gardeners need to be patient and practical, not taking on more than they can comfortably execute and maintain in the time they have. The beauty of a small, perfectly kept flower garden will far exceed the beauty of an acre of garden that is disorganized and poorly maintained.

♦ *A secret garden, surrounded by hedges or fences on three or four sides*. One side to the garden could be the house, allowing for a beautiful view out the windows. More and more people are enclosing the front of their houses with hedges and fences to provide privacy and more space for gardens. They are also discovering that perennial flower gardens and perennial groundcovers can be more interesting—and less work—than a lawn.

♦ *A garden at the edge of a pond or pool, reflected in the water to double your pleasure*. There are many kits on the market with plastic liners or formed ponds that can be installed easily in a small space by a home-owner. Water gardens are no longer reserved for people with large pocketbooks or large properties.

♦ *An island garden, a garden viewed on all sides and meant to be walked around*. An island garden can take on various geometric shapes: oval, round, half-moon, or kidney shape, to name a few. The center can be strengthened as a focal point by a flowering shrub, fountain, birdbath, sundial or small flowering tree.

♦ *A corner garden*. There is no easier place to begin. The shape itself is interesting, and what can be better than wraparound flowers?

♦ *A border*. One of the most common styles, the easiest to design, install, and maintain, is the garden border. This does not mean that it needs to be boring or uninspired. It is simply the most practical place for a new gardener to start. A border is always backed by a hedge, wall, fence, house, or any other physical barrier that can act as a backdrop to frame and direct attention to the garden. Borders have been built anywhere from 2 yards long and 1 yard wide, to 100 or more yards long and 8 or more yards wide. A border can be scalloped, curved, or straight-edged.

The important thing is not the size of the garden you wish to plant, but that the sizes of the plants are in scale with the garden. Decide what fits best in your yard, and then you are ready to begin.

Primula japonica
happily blooms in such moist places as along the side of this pond.

THEME GARDENS

A predominately white border at Old Westbury Gardens glows at dusk, reflecting the moonlight.

Winter Garden

A winter garden is fairly new to gardeners in America, although in China they have been grown for centuries. The elements of a winter garden vary depending on climate. Gardeners lucky enough to live in southern climates, in Florida or California for example, can have flowers in bloom year 'round. But, then again, these gardeners aren't greeted by bulbs in the spring as more northern gardeners are.

In northern gardens, you can create winter interest. There are perennials like Sedum 'Autumn Joy' that start with green flower heads in July, gradually turn pink in August, reddish in September, and stay a reddish brown color throughout the winter. They look wonderful capped with snow and even when they are snowed under, when they sculpt mounds of snow into shapes.

Some of the larger grasses or asters can be left at the end of the season to dry, too. We know of one adventursome gardener who spray-painted her dried grasses and perennial stalks for winter interest; while we don't recommend this, we do commend her imagination. Hellebores will bloom in January, February, and March (depending on how far north you live). Snow and frost don't bother them.

Even when the style of garden is decided, you have lots of creative flexibility. That a garden can reflect the personality of the gardener is often its chief attraction. Sometimes it is helpful to think in terms of a "theme" when planning a garden. A theme can be as simple as a color scheme, whether it be blue and white, purple and orange, or a single color. A theme can serve a specific purpose, such as attracting your favorite wildlife, say, hummingbirds or butterflies. Imagine an old-fashioned garden with plants that grandmother loved, or going back a little further, a colonial garden, a Shakespearian garden, or a Biblical garden. Imagine gardens of edible flowers or flowers that fascinate children. A moonlight garden enhances the pleasures of relaxing or dining outdoors in the evening. Nothing can match the beauty of a moonlight garden, all-white flowers that catch and reflect the light of the moon.

Fragrance gardens flaunt scents of many different sorts. The sometimes overpowering fragrance of lilies can carry as far as a neighbor's yard, and if planted by the back door, can fill the house. The subtle fragrance of *Dianthus* can be smelled only up close; put a miniature arrangement of *Dianthus* by your bedside to greet your morning with a sweet remembrance of the garden.

Fragrance in the garden was particularly important in days gone by, when frequent bathing and indoor plumbing were scarce. Like perfume, the fragrance of a garden could disguise less-than-desirable odors. Today the power of fragrance in the garden seems overlooked. But if you sit in a garden with sweet-scented *Clematis paniculata* blooming, your senses will awaken to the wonderful pleasures of a garden of fragrance.

You might plan a family garden, incorporating fragrant cutting flowers for mom, lamb's ears for the children (almost fuzzy to the touch), white flowers for evening, a few plants favored by butterflies, and anything else your heart desires. In taking this approach, hold the garden together by studying the principals of good design, coordinating colors, textures, and repetition of shapes to unify the garden. You don't want so many parts that there isn't a whole.

You are now ready to select the perennials. List the perennials that match your site and color requirements by season, including their heights and colors, on paper. If, after designing your plan, you discover the plants you want are too expensive to buy all at once, you can plant some in spring, a few more in fall, and more again the next spring. In the meantime, you can fill in "holes" with easy-care, economical annuals. A dollar packet of annual seed can cover a wide section of ground.

CHOOSING PERENNIALS

If you're a new gardener, you might want to start with the easiest and least fussy perennials. All plants require some attention, but not necessarily weekly or even monthly attention. Make sure you know how much care is required for the perennials you select. Decide where and for what purpose you want to use them, and choose varieties suited to your climate. In a large border, they can provide colorful, seasonal accents against a background of shrubs. Consider them as a groundcover under trees or on sunny slopes, in a rock garden, or formal bed, or as a naturalized planting.

The "Perennials Characteristics Chart" (page 86) will help you find the perennials which suit your needs—and the demands of the site—by season. Whenever planning the number of plants for the garden, always peer a little into the future, envision the finished picture, anticipating their growth and planning accordingly. Different perennials grow at different rates, and take up varying amounts of space.

Determine whether the area to be planted receives full sun (all day), sun for part of the day, dappled sun, or no direct sun at all. What kind of soil does it have? It is important to analyze the site before you select your perennials. Don't force plants to tolerate conditions in which they won't thrive. Planted in a favorable environment with the right sun and soil conditions, any plant requires less care. In the "Plant Portraits"

(page 35), we explain whether a plant needs sun or tolerates partial shade. A given plant might perform in partial shade, but will not be at its best. If you put plants in places that do not furnish the conditions and sunlight they need, you will be disappointed. They will be dwarfed, with scanty bloom, or scraggly.

Don't despair if the plant you long for will not grow in your garden. There are many perennials that love shade, wet feet, drought, clay, sand, or sun. In a lifetime of meeting new perennials, most will be acquaintances, a chosen few will become friends.

Every region of the country has a wealth of native plants, and these plants should be planted more freely in regional gardens than they currently are. Remember: These are the natives, the proven perennials for your area. Many plants die because they are not intelligently planted or cared for. By starting with the information in the "Plant Portraits" (page 35), you can avoid mistakes.

The trick is to continue to learn from your plants. Watch them over the years and note how they perform in different weather conditions, how they fight off pests and diseases, when they bloom best; when they do not perform well and when they need to be divided, fertilized, or watered. If you look closely, you will see that your plants have many ways of expressing what they want and need.

Perennials can be purchased in many forms. Burpee offers young plants greenhouse-grown from seed (in a few cases, from cuttings), shipped at the proper time for spring planting in your area. Some varieties can be found as mature clumps, bare-rooted and dormant after a season of growth in the field. Other perennials are sold only as field-grown plants, shipped dormant, and bare-rooted in spring and fall; these are grown from root divisions of mature plants, and they cost a bit more because they are tended longer.

Larger, potted perennials are available from your local nursery at the appropriate season for enjoying them—right before or when they are in flower. Acquiring the plant in flower is an advantage if you aren't quite sure what the flowers would look like.

Finally, the seeds of most perennials are offered at garden centers. Most need to be started indoors under lights (or on a draft-free, sunny windowsill) in early spring, or outdoors in summer for bloom the following year. Growing perennials from seed is more work—and less sure—than buying plants, but you'll have the added pleasure of nurturing them and watching them grow. It's an economical alternative when many plants are wanted, too. Be aware, however, that most perennials started from seed won't bloom until the second year in your garden. Check the "Plant Portraits" for information on individual perennial species.

DESIGNING A PERENNIAL GARDEN

PLAN ON PAPER

More so than for any other garden, it is important to do a sketch on graph paper when designing a perennial garden. The step usually skipped by beginning gardeners is the making of a general working plan. Without a plan, you take a chance that decisions made on impulse will be right. Guessing can be costly, disappointing, discouraging, and a waste of time and effort.

Measure your existing garden area and draw it on graph paper using the standard scale of landscape architects, ¼ inch to 1 foot (an easy scale with which to work). Use arrows to show the directions from which you will be viewing the garden, and note where you might place garden furniture; this will help you decide where to set your favorite plants to best advantage. Mark any eyesores that need removal or that can be covered with vines or hidden by tall plants or shrubs. You might want to emphasize existing trees and shrubs that contribute to the garden picture. If they are flowering shrubs or trees, note the season they bloom and the color of the flowers. You can draw more attention to them by adding flowering perennials that will complement them and bloom at the same time.

Use an easily erasable pencil or lay tracing paper over your existing garden plan. Now is the time to dream and experiment. Draw different shapes of gardens and see what you like best. Try it all, but only on paper. You must be realistic about how much you can execute and the time it will take to install and maintain your garden. The first year of a perennial garden is the most work. If you have plans for more than one garden, develop them over time. Don't add another garden until you understand the needs of your existing gardens.

After you decide on a site and shape, outline the garden on the ground using a garden hose, sticks with string stretched between them or by sprinkling a line of powdered lime from a pitcher. (Lime is bright white and shows up well on grass or soil. It's also biodegradable. Lime can be a beneficial addition to the soil, raising the pH and making soil less acid, but here it is used as a convenience to help visualize a garden.) This will give you a better understanding of the size and shape of your garden and how it fits in with existing plantings and structures. If you like what you've outlined, go back and draw the garden on your original plan.

In laying out your garden on paper, plan three areas: front, middle, and back (see page 76). The plants in front will be shortest, 6 to 12 inches; plants in the middle will be 1 to 3 feet tall; and plants at the back will be 3 to 5 feet tall. The size of your garden will affect what you plant. If your garden is 4 feet or less in width, you might consider grading it higher at the back by adding from 6 inches to 1 foot of new soil, which will allow plants near the back to be seen easily; you probably shouldn't use the taller plants, like *Aster* 'Harrington's Pink' or *Lythrum* 'Morden's Pink' because their spread extends to cover a 3-foot diameter in all directions and that would bring them to the front of the border. Still, some feel they can be interesting planted

A perennial border is usually designed with the tallest perennials at the back. Here the stateliest flowers draw the eye back over the fence to a second planting of foxgloves.

in a small garden as an accent. There really are few rules, and you must trust your common sense and what pleases you.

For any border, plant at least three plants of each kind of the smaller perennials, clumped together, and repeat the same clumps two or three times in the border for continuity and rhythm. Small plants, planted singly, tend to look lost or disappear entirely. If your garden is large, consider planting in fives, sevens, twelves, or more. You want the garden to look full and lush, not sparse. When you plant one iris here and another over there and a third on the far side, the eye is pulled from one to the other and doesn't really see the beauty of the iris as much as it would if they were clumped together to reinforce shapes and colors. It is better to plant a limited variety of plants and more of each kind, than one or two plants each of many varieties. You don't want a hodgepodge effect.

The more formal the design, the more it needs to be maintained to look presentable. An informal design can have a lived-in look, where plants sprawl rather than standing staked and seed pods remain on stems among flowers in bloom. With a more random placement, it doesn't

distract from the beauty of the garden if one flower clump is not quite up to par.

Island beds are easily accessible, but you must plan how you can reach into larger garden beds and borders. If your border is more than 6 feet wide, put a path along the back between the background plants and the barrier. When the plants have grown it won't show, but you will be able to work in the garden from front or back without stepping in it too much or on the plants.

Every garden bed shape offers virtually endless possibilities. Let's look at a border with

a common shape, a rectangular area usually set back against a fence, a house, at the end of a lawn, or the edge of a property, and let's imagine it in various locations with different requirements. This border is 12 feet long and 4 feet wide; let's add 2 feet in the center and at each end to allow us to soften the lines with curves. Now let's consider the garden two ways: in a sunny spot and in partial shade (four hours of sun). The criterion for both gardens is sturdy plants that require little care and flower abundantly.

First, the "Easy Care Sunny Border" (below). All the plants

The same border, shown above in June and later in July, below.

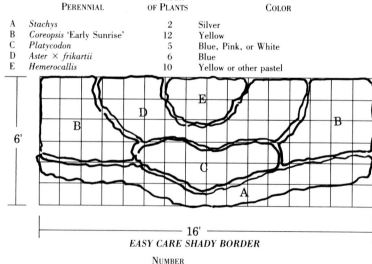

EASY CARE SUNNY BORDER

	PERENNIAL	NUMBER OF PLANTS	COLOR
A	*Stachys*	2	Silver
B	*Coreopsis* 'Early Sunrise'	12	Yellow
C	*Platycodon*	5	Blue, Pink, or White
D	*Aster × frikartii*	6	Blue
E	*Hemerocallis*	10	Yellow or other pastel

EASY CARE SHADY BORDER

	PERENNIAL	NUMBER OF PLANTS	COLOR
A	*Dicentra eximia*	24	Pink or White
B	*Hosta*	12	Variegated Foliage, White or Violet Flower
C	*Pulmonaria*	10	Variegated Foliage, Pink Flower
D	*Astilbe*	12	White, Pink, or Violet
E	*Aruncus*	1	White

chosen are trouble-free and easy to grow. Their period of bloom is another important consideration. Lamb's ear (*Stachys byzantina*) was chosen for its silver foliage, which will look good all season and tie the garden together. *Coreopsis* 'Early Sunrise', balloon flower (*Platycodon grandiflorus*) and *Aster × frikartii* were all chosen for their bloom of two to three months or longer. The daylilies (*Hemerocallis* species) will include early, mid-, and late-blooming varieties for the longest possible show from June to September. The color scheme of this border can be limited to silver, blue, and yellow or expanded with the addition of other pastel colors among the daylilies and the *Platycodon*.

For the "Easy Care Shady Border" (page 16) perennials were selected that, in addition to flowering in shade, have good foliage for three seasons. *Dicentra eximia* was chosen as edging because of its long, three-season bloom. The astilbe and the aruncus have similar plumes or feathery flowers and complement each other even though the aruncus is shrublike and the astilbes are only 2 feet high.

The hosta and the pulmonaria foliage can both be variegated to add light and depth to the shady border when not in flower and to highlight and halo their blooms.

This same plan might as easily have as its criterion a different theme, such as a butterfly garden, a color scheme of blue and gold, or a practical consideration of drought-tolerant perennials. Whatever you may choose as your criteria will make your garden special, giving you more pleasure because it will be more personal.

COLOR

Most of us garden for color whether it be riotous or quiet. Plan your colors well and you are on your way to a successful overall design.

If you limit yourself to two or three colors, it is quite easy to plan a garden around them. A fiery garden holds the colors of the sunset: red, orange, and yellow. A romantic garden might feature pastel pinks, blues, and purples all blending together in delicate and lacy flower shapes. (If you like, add perhaps a touch of yellow for zip and pizzazz.)

A white (moonlight) garden is a revelation. Every defect is concealed, the soft white-on-white blending together. The long, fragrant trumpets of lilies, spires of foxgloves, a milky way of Japanese anemone stars, snowballs of phlox and peonies, or a sea foam of boltonia, all their loveliness is enhanced by the night.

Some colors are especially noteworthy. Red is always an exclamation point; it stands out from its neighbors and draws attention to itself. The brilliant red cardinal flower (*Lobelia cardinalis*), for example, stands by itself in Nature's garden, often rising beside a stream or pond, as it loves wet feet and enjoys the reflection of its beauty in the water. It can look pitifully out of place in a garden, if not clumped together and used particularly as an accent plant. The same can be said of the brilliant scarlet of Oriental poppies, which clashes with or eclipses other flowers.

Association counts for much among plants. Without the proper companions, a flower's beauty can be minimized, dwarfed, hidden, or turned downright ugly because of clashes with its neighbor. White is a color that can act as a peacemaker, for example, when planted between neon orange and pink. It can also wash out the color of the flower next to it, though, and dilute the intended impact of such soft colors as pale pink and delicate yellow. Blue will lengthen the distance from the back of the border to the front, making your garden seem larger. Red and yellow both foreshorten the garden picture and seem to come forward, appearing closer than they really are.

Don't forget that green is a color too. There is nothing like a quiet, restful, shady green spot to raise the spirits. Mother Nature most often uses green as the peacemaker, the arbitrator that knits warring colors together and brings peace and harmony to a garden of riotous color. Green can divide warring groups; even colors that might otherwise scream are made pleasing when separated by broad stretches of green.

Native American Perennials

America has a rich horticultural heritage. Many of the plants that grace the finest gardens throughout the world originated here. When you garden with native plants, you increase the chances that your selection will be "at home," that it will take to its surroundings, thrive, and require less attention than would plants grown out of their natural environment.

Many native American perennials go unappreciated by Americans and are left out of our gardens.

Joe-Pye weed, goldenrod, and ironweed, for example, all grow freely along our roadsides in various parts of the country. European nurserymen have imported and domesticated them, teaching them proper behavior through hybridizing and selection, and are now exporting them back to us. Look again at the plants growing naturally in your region. There is beauty in simplicity and familiarity. Invite some of our native plants into your garden.

Green comes in many different shades and textures, too: the furry, silvery green of stachys to the shiny green of peony leaves; the light green filigree leaves of ferns to the dark green leaves of bergenias; the dark green grasslike foliage of liriopes to the quilted and puckered light green to blue-green broad leaves of hostas. Many perennials have a brush stroke of cream on their leaves. These variegated varieties can light up a shady spot and add interest to a sunny spot.

Sharp contrasts are not usually pleasing, although there are always exceptions to every rule. Deep purple and bright orange are a wonderfully vibrant pairing for gardeners who want a knock-'em-dead spot of color that shows up at a distance.

If you're concerned that by limiting your garden to two or three colors you're limiting the choice of plants and varieties, don't be! Varying flower shapes and plant forms adds interest and variety. Surround the solid trumpet shape of the lily with the delicate lacy flower of *Thalictrum*, or repeat the spiky plumes of *Cimicifuga* with the spiky plumes of astilbe or aruncus. Consider long-necked buttons, the billowy, spilling sprays, the curved, the straight, the open, the closed, the single, the double. The variety of flower shapes seems endless.

If organizing color and design together seems too complicated for you this year, start by planting out masses of single flowers, either in mixed or single colors. Plan a different area for each season, so that when one area is in bloom, another will be napping in the landscape. This approach, though simple, can be effective and beautiful. Make sure you don't plant your plants in uptight rows, marching in single file along your property edge or around your house. Soften the effect by massing and clumping many plants together. Avoid masses of flowers planted in a thoughtless hodgepodge of warring colors like a crazy patchwork quilt. Careless combinations can result in happy accidents, but most likely will be a misuse of plants.

Above: A bold planting of pink astilbes can be simple and effective planted along the border of a property.

COMBINING WITH PERENNIALS

Annuals, perennials, shrubs, roses, and bulbs were not intended by Mother Nature to stand alone in gardens. All enhance the beauty of one another. One will nicely fill in where the other leaves off, making for a more beautiful garden. We consider only perennials in this book because the world of garden plants is so large; even the exclusive world of perennials would fill volume after volume, leaving much to be discovered.

There are special advantages to every category of plant. The more you learn about each category, the richer and more varied your garden can be. There is no law that says roses or flowering shrubs can't be part of a perennial garden! In fact, they complement perennials.

Roses, normally finicky flowers, often are susceptible to fewer diseases when planted singly and mixed with perennials.

First-year perennials are small and don't like to be crowded while they are establishing themselves. Because annuals are mostly shallow-rooted (due to their one season of growth) and are not much bothered by crowding, they can be planted among

WINNING PLANT COMBINATIONS

Plant combinations work for the same reasons a garden design works.
Color is the single most important element holding partnerships together.

Yellow Coreopsis verticillata and blue Perovskia complement each other in shape and color.

Light pink phlox and dark rose Aubrieta bloom side by side in April.

From front to back: Stachys byzantina 'Silver Carpet', sedum 'Autumn Joy', and rudbeckia.

Combinations of the different varieties of columbine can be attractive.

Rudbeckia 'Goldsturm' blooms alongside the annual Mexican sunflower.

The burgundy foliage of sedum 'Ruby Glow' complements the dwarf shrub Spiraea 'Goldmond'.

Blue Platycodon grandiflorus blooms with sedum 'Autumn Joy'. Both perennials will bloom together for several months.

The yellow, double round flowers of the perennial coreopsis 'Early Sunrise' bloom almost as long as the spiky blue flowers of the annual Salvia farinacea.

The solid silvery foliage of Stachys handsomely balances the delicate annual Linaria maroccana.

young perennials to make the garden look full—without crowding the perennials' roots. So many annuals can give an immature perennial garden a full, lush look, abundant with flowers. The annuals will be killed by frost, and most will not reseed to return the following year when your perennials will be larger, filling in much more effectively the holes where the annuals were. Annuals can also be used as edging for a perennial garden. They can provide three or more months of bloom (depending on your climate).

Opposite, top: The April blooms of daffodils tucked in, around, and under hosta.
Bottom: The dying foliage of the daffodils is covered by luxuriant hosta.

THE ABSENTEE GARDENER

Gardening is like any endeavor: The more you put into it, the more you get out of it. A garden takes care, nurturing, and even love to perform at its best. There are periods in everyone's life when the amount of discretionary time is limited—for whatever reason. There are, fortunately, plants that tolerate a wide range of conditions and will give a wonderful performance with only a little care. The kinds of plants are limited but the varieties themselves offer a wide range of colors and sizes. The perennials marked "easy" in the "Plant Portraits" (page 35) are the ones you should consider if your time is limited.

For the gardener who wants many gardens, it is best if some of the areas planted require little care and upkeep. Such areas could include ones difficult to maintain, such as a steep bank, sloping lawn or the grass under a tree that is hidden and grows poorly in the shade and/or is difficult to cut. Convert the area to ground-hugging perennials that, once established, ask for minimal attention throughout the year. (For the adventuresome, consider planting the whole front lawn with perennials that will not only need less care than fussy, demanding grass, but they'll also offer flowers each year.)

Many perennials work well as a groundcover alternative to a lawn, in sunny or in shady areas. After all, lawns need weekly care, large amounts of water, and vigilant patrol for weeds. If you'd like grasslike foliage, consider planting liriopes, which stay green long into the fall and flower in September, a time when gardens are habitually short of flowers. Or, mix several low-maintenance perennials together and weave them in and out, with textures and foliage a pretty complement and the flowers blooming at different times. Create a more interesting texture by mixing bergenias (with large, rounded leaves that turn bright colors in the fall and stay on the plant well into spring) with such smaller-leafed variegated perennials as lamiums, pulmonarias, hostas and liriopes. Here, too, the flowers are a bonus.

For sunny spots, use stachys for large, lamb's-ear-shaped, furry, silver foliage, and cerastiums for small, delicate, furry-silver foliage. Both tolerate heat and drought. Coreopsis and rudbeckias, both with daisylike flowers, enjoy long bloom and are rarely bothered by pests or disease.

With spiky blooms, tiarellas and astilbes light up any area and are a good contrast to low, ground-hugging perennials. Alternate the ground-huggers with those that reach for the sky, the variegated with the plain, the broad-leafed with

Perennial Gardening in Frost-free Areas

In such areas as southern California, southern Florida, and along the Gulf Coast, most winters pass without the occurrence of frost or a hard freeze. In these subtropical climates especially, choose perennials that adapt well to these special conditions. Some of the plants that require cold winters can be grown in frost-free areas as annuals, by starting seeds early in the year and discarding the plants at the end of the blooming season. The plants are discarded because they won't come into bloom again without going through a dormant period.

On the other side of the coin, many other plants will survive for more than one year in a subtropical area, but are not suitable as perennials in other parts of the country. These are the tender perennials that are grown in frost-bitten climates as annuals; in the Burpee catalog these plants appear with the notation; "Grow as annuals." They include species of Antirrhinum, Artemisia, Browallia, Coleus, Impatiens, Nicotiana, Statice, Thunbergia, and Vinca. In subtropical climates these plants will eventually wear themselves out, but before then you'll have had many months of glorious bloom.

Layering the Garden with Bulbs

There are ways to "squeeze" lots of flowers into a small garden without actually overcrowding them. The general term for this is "layering," planting at different depths around and under perennials. Spring-blooming bulbs like daffodils, puschkinias, anemones and hyacinths take very little space, then go dormant from June on, so they are not depleting the soil and competing with perennials in their need for nutrients and water. Hybrid tulips, traditionally thought of as annuals as they do not return year after year, will indeed reliably bloom year after year if planted deeper than the 6 inches usually suggested on the instructions that come with the bulbs. About 10 inches, with good drainage, is preferred. Darwin hybrid tulips have been known to return for a minimum of five years, if planted 10 inches deep. This is ideal for the perennial gardener because they're deep enough so as not to interfere with surface digging for planting perennials.

Fall-blooming bulbs like Colchicum species, Lycoris species and Crocus speciosus send up leaves in the spring, die back in June, and are dormant until they send up their naked (absent of leaves) flowers in late summer and fall. They can be planted between summer-blooming perennials, to alternate using the same garden space. They add color in spring and fall at a time when the fewest perennial flowers are in bloom.

Summer-blooming lilies look better when growing up through the outer leaves of a bushy perennial such as a gypsophila or a thalictrum. With their bare bottoms, these lilies look almost naked growing alone. Because of their height, they are usually put at the back of the border so the perennials growing in front hide their bases. The small, delicate flowers of thalictrum and gypsophila surround the large trumpet shapes of the lilies in a sort of halo.

the delicate filigree-leaved, the spiky with the flat-flowered, the silver "furry"-foliaged with the deep green, shiny-leaved. Always throw in a fragrant perennial for an added gift to the senses. Alternating the repetition of colors, textures, and shapes enhances the landscape and harmonizes diverse elements to create unity. This principle applies equally to a small area under a tree and a large border.

Plan the flowering of your perennials for a time when you'll enjoy it most. Plant epimediums, tiarellas, and bergenias for early spring bloom, daylilies and hostas for long summer bloom, and *Dicentra eximia* or *Coreopsis* 'Early Sunrise' for summer-long bloom. Liriopes and Japanese anemones will end the season with fall bloom.

There are some tall, showy perennials that stand up to tough, uninviting situations. Among the most frequently used are daylilies (*Hemerocallis* species), which can be naturalized like wildflowers, planted in a shady corner or to form their own island bed and serve as a focal point for your yard. Once planted and established, they can be all but forgotten because they virtually take care of themselves. The variety of colors and bicolors of daylilies continues to expand. There are short ones, 18 inches, and tall ones, 4 feet. Each flower blooms only for a day, but another flower is waiting in the wings. The result is continuous bloom for many weeks.

Breakthroughs in breeding have given us the dwarf daylily 'Stella de Oro' that blooms for three months. With careful planning and selection, you can group a number of daylily plants together that, blooming successively, will give three months of continuous bloom.

Hostas are another easy-care perennial, very useful in a shady

GROUND-HUGGING PERENNIALS FOR PARTIAL SHADE

Ajuga species*	*Liriope* species
Bergenia species*	*Pachysandra* species*
Dicentra eximia species*	*Phlox stolonifera*
Epimedium species*	*Primula* species
Ferns*	*Pulmonaria* species
Hosta species	*Vinca* species*

GROUND-HUGGING PERENNIALS FOR FULL SUN

*Ceratostigma plumbaginoides**	*Liriope* species
	Nepeta species
Cranesbill geraniums*	*Pachysandra* species*
Hypericum species*	*Potentilla* species*
Iberis species	*Sedum* species
Lamiastrum species*	*Stachys* species
Lamium species*	*Tiarella* species*
Lavandula species*	*Vinca* species*

*Not included in "Plant Portraits," though highly recommended.

---

area. A showy perennial succeeding with little care almost anywhere, North to South, East to West, this hardy plant is more adaptable than any other to almost any soil and climate.

This does not mean that you simply plop hostas—or any other easy-care perennials—in the ground and forget about them. They will probably bloom. But give them, like all your plants, the careful soil preparation that assures years of good plant growth. Soil structure can't be successfully corrected without digging and replanting, so plant these long-lived perennials right the first time. A little more time spent at the planning and planting stages will save you time and energy later on.

It has been said that a weed is a good garden plant in the wrong place. Minimize weeding. Weeding is one of the few gardening tasks that few gardeners relish, but weeds left unchecked will ruin the appearance of your garden bed and, if they are tough enough, will beat up and crowd out the flowers you really want. Mulching is one solution that will control the weeds, but the mulch needs to be replenished periodically to keep the soil from sprouting weed seeds. Plant your perennials close enough together so that, at maturity, they will cover the ground between them; the absence of light will help prevent weeds from sprouting.

When caring for your garden, concentrate on different areas for different seasons. An area planted with daffodils, scillas, crocuses, and other spring bulbs only needs a sprinkling of slow-release 5–10–5 fertilizer each fall. A planting of peonies will bloom for only two or three weeks (depending on the variety), but the foliage, if pruned and shaped as a 2- to 3-foot hedge, can look good most of the summer with only watering.

Plant billowy masses of different kinds of astilbes, planning for bloom over two months. The astilbe plumes dry well and are even interesting as they change from red, white, or pink to beige, brown, or reddish-brown. Left on the plants, they add to the winter landscape.

THE BEHAVIOR OF PLANTS

Some plants crawl, some walk, some run, some leap, some climb, and still others charge around, knocking down anything in their way. Some garden writers have called the chargers "thugs." Make sure you understand the habits of your plants before you plant them (we note habits in the "Plant Portraits," page 35). The crawlers are those plants slow to form clumps and that need room to grow because they can't fight off a thug. The gas plant (*Dictamnus albus*), a crawler, is a wonderful, long-lasting perennial, but it needs three or more years to flower—and longer to form a decent-size clump. Once established, it is not a delicate plant; if it were, it never would have been a favorite of our great-great-grandmothers who had endless household and garden chores and no patience for demanding, temperamental plants. This crawler is a plant worth waiting for. Be considerate of your crawlers; they will repay you. Surround them with annuals or other non-invasive plants that will not try to choke them.

Walkers include hostas, daylilies, peonies, and similar plants that increase naturally at an easy pace, faster if you dig and divide them, never really threatening surrounding plants.

The plants that run can be very useful filling in bare spots, sometimes in one season. We define them as shallow-rooted perennials that are easy to remove if they grow over, under, or around other plants into places where they aren't wanted. One gardener calls them the "greeters"—they run to other plants, surround them and then tumble off to greet another, rarely harming the plants on their way. They are plants with habits that grow and spread between others, gradually covering any bare ground and knitting the bed together. As they grow around and fill in between other plants, they give continuity, rhythm, and design to the landscape.

Some plants run underground and leap up several feet in different directions from the mother plant. *Lysimachia clethroides* is

one of these. It is hard to remove because the roots are tough, strong, and deep. If you leave a section of root, another plant will easily grow from it. Since it is beautiful, with white gooseneck flowers waving in the breeze or reflecting the moonlight, plant it—but in an area next to an artifical boundary that can halt it: a sidewalk, garage, or driveway will keep it from crowding out its neighbors.

PLANT BEHAVIORS

CRAWLERS

Dictamnus species
Heuchera species
Liatris species
Platycodon species
Scabiosa species
Trollius species

GREETERS

Ajuga species
Brunnera macrophylla
Clematis species
Cranesbill geraniums
Lamium species
Lathyrus species
Vinca species
Viola species

THUGS

Aegopodium podagraria
Cerastium species
Coronilla varia
Lysimachia species
Lythrum species
Monarda species

A container of the annual heliotrope is tucked in a shady border of hosta and daylilies.

Criteria for easy-care perennials: Some perennials meet all of these requirements, others will meet a few. Consider, for instance, that perhaps you would rather have a plant that tolerates drought, and you wouldn't mind having to stake it. Take all of the following characteristics into consideration when deciding which plants to use. Features of easy-care perennials:

1. *Don't need staking*

2. *Long bloom period*

3. *Good disease and pest resistance*

4. *Don't need to be divided regularly*

5. *Don't need winter protection*

Opposite: Assorted species of ground-hugging hosta, selected to include gold, variegated, and deep green foliage, grow between a shady path and a fence. On the left, Ceratostigma plumbaginoides *is backed by astilbe.*

THE PERENNIAL PLANTING AND GROWING GUIDE

SITE PREPARATION

When preparing a new bed, keep in mind that perennials want the same things you do: a comfortable bed, good food and water, fresh air, and shelter from wind, extreme cold, and extreme heat. You will expect your perennials to live and perform in the same place for many years, so prepare the spot well for their lifetime. Long-lived perennials depend on your initial soil preparation to help them grow and flourish. If you prepare the soil to the best of your ability and resources now, you will save time, money, and energy later. It is as simple as that. A healthy soil grows a healthy plant, and a healthy plant can discourage disease and fight insects. Later, when the plants are established, you can only supplement the nutrients on the soil surface.

After you have chosen your garden site, mark the boundaries of your garden as directed on page 15. Next, remove anything that is growing on your chosen site, being especially thorough in pulling up weeds. Now you are ready to begin the process of layering and building a bed for your perennials. It is best if this can be done a week or more before you plant, to allow the soil to settle.

Check the drainage of your site. This is the most important part of soil preparation. If you have poor drainage, heavy rains will cut off air to your plants and drown them. Dig a hole two to three feet deep. You will see that the soil changes as you dig deeper. The top few inches are made up of topsoil, usually the color of dark chocolate. This is the best soil in your garden, full of nutrients because it contains newly composted organic matter—leaves, pine needles, annual plants—anything that has decomposed. The composition of the next layer varies, depending on where you live. It is either a sandy or clay soil, or something in-between.

Squeeze a handful of wet soil. If it holds together well, you have clay. If it falls through your fingers, you have sand. If it shows the imprint of your fingers and slowly collapses as you open your hand, your soil has the right texture. Clay soil is made up of small particles that compress into a dense mass when wet. Clay retains too much water, which is bad, but holds nutrients, which is good. Perennials planted in dense clay soil will be deprived of the air necessary for their survival or, if they can tolerate the clay enough to survive, they will be stunted. Sandy soil is made up of larger particles that allow for plenty of air, but let water and nutrients drain too quickly, depriving plants of water and nutrients. Both clay and sandy soils need help in order to become a good home for your perennials. By working compost or peat moss into either clay or sandy soil, you improve the soil condition. (Compost also provides nutrients for healthy growth.)

A soil test is a good investment when preparing soil for perennials. Soils poor in nutrients (or containing too much fertilizer, for that matter) will not give good results. It may be that your soil needs lime, and the only way to know is by having the soil tested. You can do it yourself with an inexpensive home-testing kit (available at garden

The long-blooming Nepeta *is complemented by the silvery foliage of artemisias and asters.*

Clay soil

Sandy soil

Loamy soil

centers) or you can mail a soil sample—a cup or two collected from different spots in the garden—to your county extension agent or state experiment station. Most perennials prefer a pH between 6.5 and 7.0.

The roots of most perennials grow deep. Dig the soil to a depth of 18 inches to 24 inches, and set it aside, keeping the topsoil separate. Mix one part compost or peat moss into three parts top soil. (If you use peat moss, add a slow-release chemical fertilizer, 5–10–5, following the directions on the package. Peat moss doesn't feed the soil but it improves water retention and texture.) Fill the hole with the topsoil mixture first, to feed the perennials' roots. If you removed sod from the bed site, it can be placed in the hole grass-side down to decompose and enrich your garden.

If you're preparing a large area, rent a rototiller. Run back and forth over an area, it breaks up the soil easily to a depth of 8 inches. Those 8 inches can be removed and the next layer can be rototilled.

This may sound like a bit of hard work, but remember that perennial gardens are prepared only once. Think instead about all the flowers that will come from your labor, and the pleasure they will bring you when they return every year.

COMPOST

If you set out to identify the most practical feminine personality of all time you might be tempted to name Mother Nature. Since time began, she has provided nourishment for all foliage, new and enduring, by recycling all organic matter once it has filled its purpose. Leaves, stalks of flowers and vegetables, branches and logs from fallen trees, all eventually decompose and enrich the earth, returning nutrients to the soil for use the next growing season. Gardeners call the process "composting," and though horticulturists and scientists have never been able to improve on it exactly, they have been able to speed it up. Rather than taking a year or more, composting can now be done in weeks. The advantage of this speedup is that you get more compost, the rich and enriching humus that is the finest material available for making a garden thrive and bloom. It is a material of which you cannot have too much.

Compost-making is simple.

You help Nature, and she does the work. How much you help affects the time it takes to make compost. Assemble the ingredients all at once. You'll need some carbon materials such as dry leaves, hay, straw, or seaweed and some nitrogen materials, such as grass clippings, fresh weeds, and manure. If you are really in a hurry for compost, you chop up the materials, either by hand or with a chipper or a lawn mower, in order to expose more of the compost material surface to the organisms that start the decomposition process. These organisms are Nature's work force. They work so hard that they create heat, raising the temperature of the compost. 150 degrees Fahrenheit is ideal for decomposing rapidly, reducing the material to a rich, brown humus.

As the materials decompose, the compost pile settles and reduces in size. It will be only about 40 percent of its original size in about a week. As you turn the pile, moving the mate-

rials toward the edges to the center, and occasionally giving it a thorough wetting, eventually the pile will decrease by another 40 percent. The resulting material, spread around your garden, will produce outstanding results.

If you just don't have enough time to turn the pile weekly, there is an alternative, but it will take longer. Simply pile leaves or grass clippings, leaving a concave bowl on the top of the pile to capture rain; leave the pile to decompose. Turn it once or twice a summer and let Nature do the rest, but plan on a year before you can use it in your garden. Environmentalists appreciate and endorse composting leaves and grass clippings instead of putting them into plastic bags that end up in the local landfill. Of all garbage pickup across America, 20 percent is garden refuse, mostly grass clippings and fall leaves. Think of all the money to be saved and the great gardens to be grown through composting!

One more very important item. What is the best way to contain the compost pile? There are many options. You can lay cement block about 5 feet high on three sides, using the holes in the blocks for ventilation so air can circulate through the pile; leave the fourth side open so that you can work the pile. A second option is to build four frames from 2 × 4 lumber, about 4-feet square, and cover them with chicken wire. Assemble them into a box, with the fourth side hinged so you can open the bin and work the pile. A third option is to purchase one of the commercial compost bins readily available on the market. This is more expensive, but the bins generally last for many years and reward you with good compost.

Mulching

Mulching is not new; the ancient Romans used a stone mulch to warm the soil and keep plants cool, moist, and weed-free. Even so, at Burpee we suspect the familiar art of mulching is not practiced nearly often enough.

There are many benefits to mulching. Mulch conserves soil moisture, smothers weeds and

warms the earth in the spring and keeps it cool on hot summer days. Most importantly, as organic mulch (as opposed to plastic mulch) breaks down, it feeds the soil. The only disadvantage to mulch is that it can hide slugs. A sprinkling of wood ashes or diatomaceous soil under the leaves of plants (where its off-white color will be hidden from view) will keep them in check, as will a collar surrounding each individual plant stem (see also page 79).

Mulch for perennial flower gardens should be attractive and enhance the flower colors. Remember, when selecting a mulch, that your purpose is to draw attention to the flowers, their colors, fragrance, and shapes. Don't choose a mulch that calls attention to itself.

There are lots of organic mulches from which to choose, depending on where you live and what is available. Pine needles, wood bark, small (not large) wood chips, cocoa bean shells, seaweed, seashells, buckwheat hulls, and shredded leaves are all good mulches. The difference is cosmetic, a matter of taste; they will all do the job. A soil raked clean, without mulch, will starve your plants.

What to put in the compost pile—	What not to put in the compost pile:
Remember that the smaller the pieces are, the faster they will decompose:	*cooked food*
	weeds with seed pods
shredded or whole fall leaves (first drag a lawn mower back and forth over leaves to shred, or use a leaf shredder)	*raw fish and animal remains (good compost, but they attract mice and other small animals)*
shredded bark (you'll need a wood chipper for this)	*diseased plants (the disease will spread)*
shredded twigs	*any plant material that has been treated with a herbicide or pesticide within the past three weeks*
fresh vegetable and fruit peelings	
grass cuttings	
tea leaves	
coffee grounds	
well-rotted horse or cow manure	
eggshells	
cut flowers	
salt hay*	
pine needles	

*This is made from wild grass (sold at nurseries) grown in salt water. Unlike common hay, salt hay does not contain seeds.

Mulch is the only way a gardener has to improve the soil without digging up the plants. Remember that plant food doesn't improve the soil, nor does it stay in the soil very long; it just dissolves and washes into our ground water. The most popular mulches are:

SHREDDED LEAVES: Shred autumn leaves with a leaf shredder, or run a lawn mower back and forth over a low pile of leaves. Place shredded leaves directly on the flower beds.

Left: This compost starter bin is easy to make from four 4-foot posts, set in a rectangle, wrapped in chicken wire. If the chicken wire is secured loosely on the fourth side, the bin can be opened easily for removal of compost or for working the compost pile.

PINE NEEDLES: They are very attractive, especially in shade gardens. They can simply be raked from under evergreens and spread around your plants. When used consistently, they eventually lower the pH of the soil. A sprinkling of lime mixed with the pine needles will correct this, if a soil test indicates a too-low pH.

WOOD CHIPS: The smaller the pieces, the faster they decompose and need to be replaced. All wood chips look better weathered, which can take a few weeks. Large wood chips, good under shrubs, are too bulky for use with small plants. Sawdust works well, but it breaks down quickly and must be replaced several times over a season. You can make your own wood chips by putting small branches and twigs through a chipper.

BUCKWHEAT HULLS: These are sold commercially in bags. They are very attractive, but can be expensive if you need to cover a large area. They are rather lightweight and will blow around in windy areas.

COCOA BEAN SHELLS: These are also sold commercially in bags, and make an attractive, dark-colored mulch that sets off the lighter colors in your garden. Be prepared to have your garden smell of chocolate for a week or two.

SMALL STONES OR COLORFUL GRAVEL: This mulch is widely used in Japanese gardens. The stones can leach some minerals into the soil and will of course conserve moisture, but will not break down and add humus.

Mulch should be placed around the plants approximately 3 inches thick. It will need to be replaced periodically as it breaks down. Don't put mulch around your seedlings until they are 5 inches high and firmly established. The decomposition of mulch will inhibit seed germination (good for discouraging weeds).

DIVISION

Perennials increase in beauty and number as they mature. When plantings threaten to become too large, the clumps can be divided, then replanted elsewhere in your garden, or in the garden of a friend. For the gardener who loves to share plants with neighbors and friends, perennials are a delight. Just be sure to reserve visiting rights to see your offspring in your friends' gardens.

Some perennials are easily started from root divisions or cuttings. Gardeners, being generous people, love sharing and trading their plants. Many garden clubs hold plant exchanges where members can extol the virtues of their plants while exchanging them with new friends for new plants. Or, you might try to find out who in your neighborhood is interested in gardening, so you can trade cuttings, root divisions, and information. Gardeners learn from each other. At Burpee we often get letters from customers telling us their methods and hints for successful gardening, which we gratefully pass along in our catalogs, books, and bulletins.

Perennials can be increased by division. Some plants (anchusas, for example) demand to be divided yearly or they don't perform; others are better off if divided every few years. Still another group, including peonies, daylilies, and hostas, can be divided or left alone and will still perform well. Perennials vary greatly in the amount of time they can flourish without dividing. As a rule, most perennials benefit from being divided every three to five years. Others can be divided yearly if you want to increase your stock of plants.

The methods of dividing vary. Some perennials can be divided by thrusting a pitchfork into the root and pulling the tuber apart. Others, like astilbes, need an axe to divide their tough roots. Use whatever tools are easiest for you.

When to divide perennials depends on the time of bloom. For some it is best to divide only after the flower has bloomed, not during or before blooming. Peonies, irises, violets, and daylilies can be divided while the plants are resting in August. Spring is a good time to divide most perennials; be care-

When digging up a plant (here, a hosta), get as large a root ball as possible.

Use a sharp knife to divide the root ball in half or quarters.

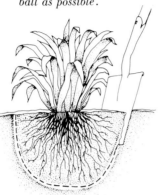
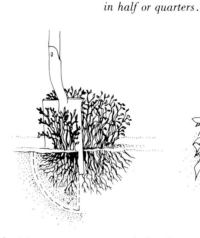

ful, because if you spade into a garden too early in the season you can injure plants you've forgotten are there. Clumps to divide in spring include phlox, penstemons, boltonias, bee balms, and Japanese anemones. Consult the "Plant Portraits" (page 35) for information on dividing particular perennials.

Above, from left to right:
The roots rarely exceed the boundaries described by the foliage above them.
Some perennials, such as astilbe, can be divided by removing only a section of the plant and leaving the rest in the ground.
After digging up daylilies, divide them by thrusting two pitchforks into the roots and pulling the tubers apart.

STAKING

Staking is the supporting of plants to keep them upright. Some plants grow so fast and are so prolific that their stalks can't hold them up. It is necessary for tall, weak-stemmed plants, plants in exposed sites and plants with large-headed flowers. Never wait until your plants are lying on the ground. Some plants always need staking and you will find them so identified in the "Plant Portraits" (page 35). Other plants don't always need it, but you can tell

that they do when they are bent over and appear to be struggling with too heavy a load.

The important thing to remember is that a proper stake is like a corset, not meant for public display. Camouflage is the password for staking. When your staking can't help but be partially visible, choose green bamboo stakes, green metal plant stakes, and green strings or twist-ems. You don't want to distract from the flower display. Too-tight staking is unattractive

and looks unnatural. Restricting a plant's movement with tight staking can cause the plant to be injured on windy days, too.

For any plant that needs staking—single-stemmed plants like delphiniums and lilies, for example—insert a rigid stick (a dowel is fine) into the ground near the stalk but far away enough to avoid contact with the roots, and secure it loosely to the stalk with ties. This will give the plant room to grow straight, yet unhampered.

Whenever possible, use green plant stakes because they blend in with the foliage.

Single-stemmed plants can be staked individually.

Bushy plants can be grown through plant hoops which give them room to sway without breaking.

Or grow them next to a fence that they can lean on; tie them loosely.

For a grouping of tall, unsteady bushy plants, you can erect a support with four stakes around the perimeter of the plants, then run string around the outside of the stakes and across from corner to corner. As the plants grow, they will hide both stakes and string with foliage. Garden catalogs and garden supply stores sell plant hoops that are easily inserted into the ground and are reuseable from year to year.

DEADHEADING

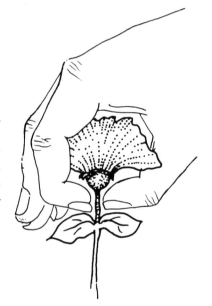

Removing spent flower blossoms from perennials will prevent the plants from directing their energy toward developing seeds. Instead, it will force them to produce more flowers, and this can greatly extend the blooming time of each individual plant. Once plants start to produce seeds, they produce fewer and fewer flowers.

TRANSPLANTING

I have been accused of having wheels on my plants because I seem to move them around so much from year to year. If I notice a plant blooming on one side of my garden that I would like to introduce to another plant on the other side of the garden, I move it. Plants, like people, can be improved by the company they keep. Moving doesn't hurt most plants, but check first in the "Plant Portraits" (page 35) to see which are homebodies and which are travelers.

The ideal day for transplanting is an overcast day when the clouds protect the exposed plant roots from the sun. If you must transplant on a sunny day, it is best to do it in early morning or late afternoon. But if the only time available is in the middle of a sunny day, you will have to be cautious. Follow these tips:

1. Don't let exposed roots sit in the sun. Strong sun will dry and kill the soft roots in a short time. You should have your hole prepared before removing the plant from its container or bed.
2. Be careful, when removing plants from their homes, that you don't damage the roots. To remove plants from containers,

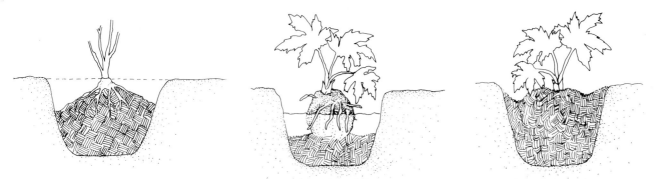

turn the container upside-down and hold the stem gently between your fingers. Tap the bottom of the container until the plant falls into your hand. If your plants are in plastic cell packs, you can push up and down on the bottom of the individual cell to loosen the roots and gently pull out the plant.

3. Prepare the hole well, digging it one and a half times the size of the root ball. Mix organic matter or compost in the bottom to give the roots nutrition and good soil to grow down into. Bone meal is the only fertilizer that can be planted in the hole with the roots; 5–10–5 fertilizer would burn the roots if it touched them directly.

4. Spread the roots evenly in the hole to give them room to grow. If you crowd them or leave them scrunched up, it will take more time and energy for the plant to straighten them out itself and get on with the business of growing and blooming.

5. After the plant is in the ground, it is best to protect it from scorching sun for a few days. If the plant is small you can put a piece of a garden blanket over it, which will cut down on the rays of the sun. You could shade a larger plant with a cardboard box or a wooden board that will cast a shadow over it for part of the day. In most cases you won't lose the plant if you don't shade it, if it has adequate water, but it will take longer to adjust to its new home and begin to grow.

6. New transplants need more water, more often, until they become established. Check on your plants daily to see that they are not drooping from too much sun or lack of water.

Grow Healthier Plants . . . Save Water, Too!

Many plants are lost and much water wasted due to improper watering. During the growing season, plants require on average one inch of rainfall per week. One inch of rainfall—easy to measure in a rain gauge—will penetrate the soil to 8 inches. If Nature provides it, fine; otherwise, the gardener must do so. Proper soil preparation, incorporating lots of organic matter into the soil, will increase the ability of the soil to retain water. Recently, excellent results have been obtained by adding a polymer, Water Grabber™, to soils, both in the garden and in containers. When mixed with garden soil it vastly increases water retention, releasing water to plants as needed; it breaks down after about three years. It is available through Burpee or at your local garden center.

The way you water is critical. The gardener who stands waving a hose around to sprinkle his garden may be doing something for his conscience, but little for his plants! Frequent and shallow watering is useless. Worse than that, it can be damaging, encouraging the formation of roots too near the surface. When you water, it should be done thoroughly, supplying water that will penetrate the soil to a depth of 8 inches at each application. Proper watering can take several hours, depending on the delivery capacity of your equipment.

Whenever possible, soaking rather than spraying equipment should be used. Soakers or drippers deliver water most effectively, wasting little to evaporation or run-off, and they don't leave water dripping on the foliage, which can make plants susceptible to disease.

Good water is becoming more precious. Conserve water, and your valuable plants, by using it correctly!

Above, left: Spread the roots evenly on top of the mounded soil in the hole.
Center: Fill the hole with water and let soil settle.
Right: Add more soil until it reaches just below ground level to direct water to the plant's roots.

Propagation from Stem Cuttings

Generally, perennials are slow to grow from seed, not blooming until their second or third summer. Growing them from stem cuttings, on the other hand, speeds up the process. To grow from cuttings:

1. Cut a 3- to 4-inch piece of a stem that is neither new (weak) nor old (tough) from an established plant. Use a sharp knife or scissors for cutting, to avoid damaging stem tissues. Make the cut ½ inch below a node—the place where a leaf is attached to the stem, or where a pair of leaves or two or more branches come together; this ensures the cutting will have sufficient food reserves in its tissues to sustain it until it can produce roots.

2. Two sets of leaves on the cutting will help prevent wilting and promote rooting. If there are more than two sets of leaves, flower buds or even two large leaves, it is harder for the stem to stay alive as they all zap the stem's energy. Remove flower buds and excess leaves, and cut the tip half from any large leaves to help the stem focus on producing roots. The stem can be kept in water for a few days if you are not ready to plant it immediately. If you've taken the cutting from a friend's garden and won't be home for a few days, it will keep well sealed in a plastic bag with a little moisture.

3. Fill a tray or pot with moist (not soggy) rooting medium (sand, vermiculite or a mixture of peat moss and sand). Dip the node end of the stem in a rooting hormone (available at garden supply stores). The rooting hormone helps speed the growth of healthy new roots. Make a hole in the rooting medium with a pencil. This hole should be wider than the cutting stem, so the stem won't be damaged when placed in the hole (and the hormone powder won't rub off). Stand the stem in the hole, node end first; roots will grow out of the node. Gently firm the planting medium around the stem.

4. Cover the stem and tray (or pot) with a plastic bag and close it; this will keep the atmosphere moist. Rooting is promoted by moisture and warmth, particularly bottom heat. Place the tray in a warm (70 to 80 degrees Fahrenheit) spot. You might set it on top of the refrigerator or a warm—not hot—radiator, or in a cold frame in partial sun (not full sun, which would scorch the cutting).

5. Different perennials root at different rates. As long as your stem cuttings are healthy, they will eventually root. If you notice rot or mildew, separate the affected stem from other cuttings and discard it.

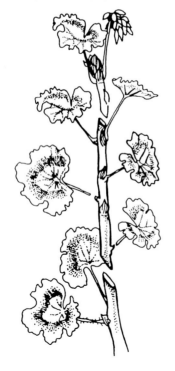

Make a cut about ½ inch below a node.

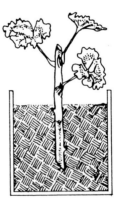

Gently firm the rooting medium around the stem.

A clear plastic covering ensures a moister environment for the cutting.

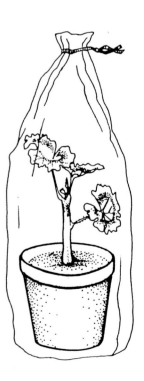

Putting the Garden to Bed for the Winter

Northern gardeners have the special problem of protecting their plants from frost, snow, and the otherwise bleak, harsh conditions of winter. Perennials die back to the ground in winter, store food in their roots, and remain dormant until the spring rain and warming sun wake them. Some perennials (for example, coralbells) resent being tucked in with winter blankets which hold the wet and cold of winter longer. But most perennials appreciate the gardeners' consideration and will be stronger and greener sooner because of the winter blankets.

In laying down a blanket, the gardener is preventing the ground from repeatedly freezing and thawing over the course of winter, confusing the plants during a warm spell into starting to grow or, worse yet, heaving them out of the ground. After any thaw, take a walk around the garden to see whether any roots or bulbs are lying on top of the ground. You can press them back into the ground, without any loss, if you find them before the ground freezes again.

Spread a winter blanket after the ground has frozen hard. Cover your plants with salt hay, straw, evergreen boughs, shredded leaves, or any other protective covering that won't become compact and prevent water and air from reaching them. (Unshredded leaves tamp down and form a solid mass on the soil that prevents water from draining into the soil. On the other hand, boughs cut from Christmas trees work beautifully, and are a wonderful way to recycle Nature's gifts.)

Snow is another cozy garden cover, although it works best when salt hay, straw, or boughs are already in place as well. If you're shoveling your driveway or walk, heave the snow on the garden—the higher the pile, the better the protection. Note that in years when the snow cover is light in northern gardens, the loss of perennials is higher. Important: If you use salt on walkways and driveways, be careful that the salt doesn't wash onto the garden where it will be harmful.

Keep a lookout during warming weather for erosion from melting snow. You don't want a stream running through your perennial bed, washing away precious topsoil, opening the ground, and exposing roots to excessive water.

Remove winter blankets in early spring when the season of hard, deep frost is over. All of the winter coverings can be added to the compost pile.

PLANT PORTRAITS

More than eighty perennials are discussed in detail in this chapter. They were chosen for their popularity, easy culture, and availability. Start your garden by becoming acquainted with these plants and, as your friendship grows with one plant, it will lead you to another, and another. As your interest in perennials grows, so will your garden.

The plants that follow are listed under their botanical (Latin) names and cross-referenced by their common names. Having the plant information you want listed under the scientifically correct name avoids confusion and misunderstanding. The system of botanical nomenclature was founded by the Swedish botanist Carolus Linnaeus. Every known plant has a first name, the genus (indicated by the first Latin word), a grouping of plants with similar characteristics. Every plant has a second name, too, the species (the second Latin word), which further identifies shared qualities of lesser importance. Although common names are easier to pronounce, they can be confusing because many different flowers grown in different parts of the country have the same common name. Using botanical names is the one way to be sure of having the correct cultural information.

PLANT PORTRAIT KEY

Here is a guide to the symbols and terms we used throughout this section.

Latin name of the perennial is in boldface italic.

Phonetic pronunciation of the Latin name is in parentheses.

Common name of the perennial is in boldface type.

The average hours of sun needed per day is indicated by symbols. The first symbol is what the plant prefers, but the plant is adaptable to all conditions listed.

○ *Sun*—Six hours or more of strong, direct sunlight per day.
◗ *Part shade*—Three to six hours of direct sunlight per day.
● *Shade*—Two hours or less of direct sunlight.
Symbols for:
  ◆ *Drought-resistant*
  ✸ *Heat-lover*

✳ *Cool-weather perennial*
❦ *Long-lasting cut flower*
❀ *Long bloomer—6 weeks or longer*

Grade of Difficulty— Perennials that take the least amount of care are identified as "easy." These plants are a good choice for beginning gardeners with little time.

Native American are the plants that were growing on the American continent when the pilgrims arrived. Many plants that are native to America are also native to other countries around the world.

Heights are for normal growth, but perennials with very fertile soil and a longer growing season could grow taller. Conversely, with poor growing conditions, the plant could be shorter.

Zones Check "The USDA Plant Hardiness Map" (page 85), based on average annual temperatures for each area—or zone—of the United States to see what zone you live in. Some perennials

Iberis, white columbines, and roses bloom together in a corner garden.

Acanthus spinosus

grow better in northern gardens, Zones 3 through 7, some better in southern gardens, Zones 8 through 10, and a few will grow anywhere. Every plant portrait lists the zones best for that plant.

Cultural Information Plants' preferences and information how best to grow your plants are given here. We recommend the easiest and best methods of increasing your number of plants. Some perennials are best grown from seed, others from division or stem cuttings.

Recommended Cultivars We have recommended particular varieties or cultivars of perennials when there are many choices available, to help you understand the differences among cultivars and to inform you about exceptional ones.

Acanthus (a-KANTH-us) **bear's breech** Easy ○ ◑
Zones: 8 to 10
Height: 3 to 4 feet; dwarf, 18 inches
Colors: Lavender, creamy white, or rose with purplish markings
Characteristics: Acanthuses are famous for the shape and simple beauty of their leaves, the inspiration for the carvings that decorate ancient Greek corinthian columns. Their size, decorative foliage, and luxuriant growth—quickly forming a fountainlike shape—make acanthuses good choices for massing as a stately landscape accent or planting singly in perennial borders in the place of shrubs. Their immense, glossy, dark green leaves and tall, muted blue flower spikes are arresting, even when seen from a distance. They are drought-tolerant

Achillea filipendula
'Gold Plate'

and evergreen, features that make them popular on the West Coast, and can be grown in Zone 7 with protection (but sometimes refuse to flower).

Acanthus mollis 'Latifolius' is recommended for large sculptural groups. *Acanthus perringii* is a dwarf variety, 18 inches high, ideal for small perennial gardens.

Cultural Information: These spiky plants grow best in moist, rich soil with good drainage, but do well in dry, sandy soil too. They prefer filtered sun and moist soil in hot climates but will grow in full sun with drier soil in cooler climates. In excessively wet winter soils, acanthuses rot and die. In California coastal regions, their roots spread underground particularly rapidly if not confined. In northern zones, plant in warm, protected areas and mulch over for winter. Space plants 3 to 4 feet apart. Confine roots—unless you want a large stand—as they spread a considerable distance underground to form spreading clumps, like bamboo. Acanthuses rarely need division for rejuvenation but are easily propagated and divided in the spring. Any piece of a root, left underground, is capable of reproducing. Cut plants back to ground after bloom for renewal of foliage growth.
Uses: Landscape plant, back of the border.

Achillea (a-KIL-lee-a) **yarrow** Native American Easy ○ ✳ ✿
Zones: 3 to 8
Height: 1½ to 2 feet; Achillea 'Gold Plate', 5 feet
Colors: White, yellow, pinks, red

Characteristics: Long-blooming plants, achilleas quickly establish handsome colonies in the border. They are excellent as cut flowers, lasting longer if foliage is removed from the stems. The leaves have a pungent, herbal fragrance when touched or stripped from the stems. Leaves are deep cut, fernlike and gray-green in color. Achilleas are members of the daisy family (*Compositae*), which includes many common weeds. Some varieties are rapid spreaders through basal shoots. *Achillea filipendulina*, commonly called fern-leaf yarrow, is known for its showy yellow, flat-topped, dense flower clusters measuring 3 to 5 inches across. One variety, aptly named 'Gold Plate', reaches 5 feet tall and might need staking. The new hybrid Galaxy series is available in a wider color range: soft buff yellow, light rose, reddish purple, and deep crimson red. I grow *A. millefolium* 'Fire King', a 2-foottall variety with floppy stems, next to something with a stiffer habit like blue echinops or gypsophila, and let the achillea drape over onto its neighbors. *A. ptarmica* 'The Pearl' is a good, dwarf garden variety with its double white flowers on 2-foot stems. All achilleas make fine dried arrangements.
Cultural Information: Plant achilleas 2½ to 3 feet apart, in well-drained soil in fall or late spring after danger of frost. Cut back to a few inches from the ground after flowering to help induce bushiness and more flowers. Divide every 3 to 4 years in early spring or late fall for rejuvenation. To avoid stem rot, water only moderately late in the day,

especially in moist climates. Achillea prefer soils that are not especially fertile, so avoid excessive use of nitrogen fertilizer. Although these plants are considered drought-resistant, they do appreciate a good watering during dry, hot weather. After the plants are several inches high, mulch the soil between them with compost or other material that will decompose in one season to keep weeds down and conserve moisture. Achillea are generally pest-free due to their pungent foliage and are easily grown from seed. Germination takes from 10 to 14 days; the optimum temperature is 65 to 70 degrees Fahrenheit.

Uses: Border, cutting, dried flowers.

Aconitum (a-kon-EE-tum) monkshood Moderate

◑ ○

Zones: 5 to 8
Height: 3 to 5 feet
Colors: Blue, white, pink, yellow, or bicolor
Characteristics: Wonderful for late-summer, early-fall bloom when there are very few blue flowers available. Aconitums resemble their close relatives the delphiniums but are much more reliable. These showy, hooded- or helmut-shaped flowers grow on upright spikes. Their dark green foliage consists of finger-like leaves and are an asset in the garden all summer. Cultivars of *A. napellus* bloom first, in late July. *A. napellus* 'Bicolor' shows up in light shade with its white flowers edged with China blue. *A. carmichaelii* has the darkest blue flowers, in August and September. For yellow or creamy white flowers in July, grow *A. vulparia*.

Cultural Information: Rich, moist soil is needed for growth, and they prefer part shade and cooler climates. Aconitums can be left undivided for many years; divide them in the fall after they have finished flowering. Aconitums are not easily propagated from seed, sometimes taking 18 months to germinate and 3 years to flower. Plant either tuberous roots or started plants in fall or spring. Established clumps resent transplanting. Mulch around each plant in May to help hold the moisture and keep roots cool.

Caution

All parts of this plant are poisonous and the sap is extremely toxic—be careful when handling or cutting.

Uses: Back of the border, woodland walks, shady corners.

Adam's needle; see *Yucca.*

Alcea rosea (al-KEE-a RO-see-a) hollyhock Moderate

○ ✸

Zones: 3 to 8
Height: Up to 6 feet
Colors: White, yellow, purple, red, rose
Characteristics: An old garden favorite with a long-blooming season. Usually considered a biennial in Zones 3 to 8, but may live for several years if stalks are cut off at their bases after the flowers fade. Makes an excellent screening plant to hide unsightly views, a good background companion for shorter plants. Very easy to grow, preferring a warm, sunny location sheltered from the wind. Blooms midsummer to early fall with 4-inch double flowers that are borne on wandlike stems. Alcea blooms start near the base of the stem and move upward, so that 1½ to 2 feet of each stem is covered with bloom throughout the season. The leaves are hairy, 6 to 8 inches across, borne in low clumps. Plants grow up to 6 feet in height.

Cultural Information: Will do well in almost any soil but prefers a well-drained soil with pH 6.0 to 8.0 (from slightly acid to alkaline). Plant in spring or fall in a sunny location sheltered from the wind. Try to have the soil worked up at least one week before planting.

Where winters are severe, spring planting is preferred to fall planting. Plant as soon as nursery stock is received. If planting must be delayed, place the plants in a cool, shaded area and keep the roots moist. Hollyhock seedlings are grown in a special planting mixture to promote fast growth. Do not pull this material away from the roots, but set the top of the planting material level with the soil line. Firm the soil around the plants and roots, pressing with your hands, and water well to eliminate air pockets that may form around the roots.

Space plants 18 inches apart. If planted in rows, space rows at least 3 feet apart. Some plants may require staking to support fragile stems in windy areas. Will tolerate moist conditions if soil is well-drained. Water thoroughly during hot, dry weather. Remove any seed heads that may form so plants will continue to bloom for several years. Most plants will bloom for several years in Zones 3 to 8 if stalks are cut off at the base

Aconitum napellus

Alcea rosea *'Fordhook®*
Giants'

Anchusa azurea
'Loddon Royalist'

Opposite, from top:
Anemone x hybrida
'Queen Charlotte';
Anemone x hybrida
'Alba'; Anemone
vitifolia 'Robustissima';
and Aquilegia
'McKana's Giant'.

Amsonia tabernaemontana

after flowers have faded, but they will not be as vigorous as new seedlings. Once established in the garden, plants often grow from seeds dropped during the summer. These chance seedlings should be transplanted elsewhere so as not to crowd the parent plants.

Uses: Back of the border, cutting.

Amsonia (am-SON-ee-a) blue-star Native American Easy ○ ◐ ✳ ❘

Zones: Zone 3 to 8 for *A. tabernaemontana* (wild amsonia); Zones 6 to 8 for *A. ciliata*
Height: 2 to 3 feet
Colors: Light, steely blue
Characteristics: Amsonias, with clusters of small blue stars, bloom for only two weeks in late May or early June, but the willowlike foliage is attractive all summer long and turns brilliant gold in fall. In northern climates they have been known to bloom as late as July. The individual flowers are tiny and delicate. Plants are restrained in growth, but carefree and long-lived. *A. tabernaemontana*, the wild amsonia native to the East Coast, likes a moist, fertile soil. *Amsonia ciliata*, with narrower leaves, is native to dry, open woods from North Carolina to Texas and prefers drier soil.

Cultural Information: Amsonias rarely require division. If necessary, divide in spring or fall. Plant in moist, fertile soil about 12 to 15 inches apart. As these plants bloom late in the spring, take care not to injure them when cultivating. It is best to plant in the fall because the plants bloom in the spring. They can be grown from seed sown in the fall. If sown in spring, first chill the seed for several weeks and sow when daytime temperatures reach 45 degrees Fahrenheit. Seeds sprout in three weeks.
Uses: Foliage, woodland, borders, cutting.

Anchusa azurea (an-KEW-sa a-ZEWR-ree-a) Italian alkanet, Italian bugloss Easy ○ ◐ ❘

Zones: 3 to 8
Height: 2½ to 5 feet
Colors: Purple, blue
Characteristics: Anchusas overflow with large, intense blue flowers in clusters 1 inch across, produced profusely in early summer. Their blue color and showy display rival the delphiniums. The pyramid-shaped plants can become floppy from the weight of so many flowers. The leaves are rough, tongue-shaped, covered with bristly hairs, and dark green in color. They shrink in size as they go up the plant, starting at the bottom with leaves a foot or more long, ending with leaves of a few inches long at the top. Anchusas are excellent companion plants for coreopsis or painted daisy (*Chrysanthemum coccineum*). The variety 'Loddon Royalist' won the Award of Merit at the famous Chelsea show, in England, where it was

first presented. These exceptional plants are loaded with unusually large flowers, long-lasting when cut for bouquets. Other good varieties are 'Dropmore' (especially for shady spots), 'Pride of Dover', and 'Royal Blue'.
Cultural Information: Anchusas are easily grown but not long-lived unless divided every season. The older plants produce bold, coarse foliage at the expense of bloom. If allowed to go to seed, they will reseed themselves; the seedlings, as they appear, can be transplanted to a protected area for growing on, then returned to a permanent place in the garden the following spring. Grow in rich, well-drained soil and avoid clay soil unless it has been carefully prepared. Vigilant watering is needed during periods of hot, dry weather but take care to avoid overwatering. In windy areas, stalks may need staking to keep them from breaking or blowing over. In late fall, before the ground is too hard to dig, mound 2 to 3 inches of soil directly over newly set plants to divert moisture from them in winter. Divide plants annually—they rarely bloom well for more than one season without being divided and replanted. Replenish the soil with compost when replanting. This can be done in spring or fall, and is well worth the effort.

Leaves become floppy and unattractive after flowers fade. Cut down to ground to come up again with better, fresh foliage. Seeds germinate in about fourteen days in cool temperatures of 50 to 60 degrees Fahrenheit. Seed can be sown in spring or fall. Seedlings sown in early spring mature and flower in one season. Plants can be increased by division or root cuttings.

Uses: Border, naturalize in open spaces with deciduous trees, cutting.

Anemone × hybrida

(a-NEM-o-nee HIB-ri-da) **hybrid anemone, Japanese anemone**
Easy ◐ ● ○ ❚
Zones: 5 to 8
Height: 2 to 3½ feet
Colors: White, warm rose, pink
Characteristics: Anemones are among the most beautiful of fall-blooming perennials, bridging the gap between the flowers of summer and the garden's last great fall show of chrysanthemums. Their single or double long-stemmed flowers dance above dark green, deeply lobed foliage. Excellent for cutting. Bloom season is late summer to fall frost. Anemones belong to the buttercup family (*Ranunculaceae*) and have no true petals; showy parts are petallike sepals. Plants produce a moundlike habit with branched stems.

'Honorine Jobert' and 'Alba' are varieties with single white flowers; 'Margarete' has semidouble deep, almost shocking pink flowers, and 'Queen Charlotte' has pink semidouble flowers. Many more wonderful varieties are available.

Cultural Information: Cool, humus soil, well-drained but liberally supplemented with peat moss or organic matter, is the ideal. Water liberally during hot, dry weather. Plants mature fully in two to three years. Divide anemones when the plants fail to bloom well. New plants made from root cuttings or clump di-

visions made in early spring will bloom the same year. The plants dislike being disturbed and should not be moved unnecessarily. In Zones 5 and 6, mulch plants for winter with straw or light organic matter placed on plants in the fall after the ground freezes. In addition to division of crowns, root cuttings may be made. Pieces of root taken in fall or early spring, planted in boxes of sandy loam or leaf mulch and tended in cool greenhouses will be developed enough for planting outdoors the following summer. (If no greenhouse is available, place in a cold frame.) Remove faded flowers to encourage new bloom and good plant strength. Set plants 12 to 18 inches apart when planting.

Uses: Cutting, middle to back of the border, naturalized in open woods.

Aquilegia (ak-wil-EE-jee-a)

columbine Native American
Easy ◐ ○ ✳ ❚
Zones: 4 to 8
Height: 1½ to 3 feet
Colors: Blues, pinks, reds, and yellows, most with contrasting centers
Characteristics: Columbines are graceful, multicolored flowers adorned with long spurs that nod upright above lacy, light green foliage, similar to that of Maidenhair fern. Each flower is made up of five petallike sepals set over five petals, which may be the same or a different color. The spurs are usually full of nectar, often attracting hummingbirds. Columbines are short-lived perennials, lasting about three years in the garden, but they freely self-sow when

they like their home. Columbines bloom in May and June and are good complements in form and color to species of *Iberis* and *Dicentra*. *Aquilegia canadensis* is our native woodland plant, with scarlet petals and yellow centers. 'Harlequin' is an earlier blooming variety with large flowers. 'McKana's Giant' has extra-large flowers in bright colors and bicolors. 'Nora Barlow' is an unusual fully double flower of red, pink, and green blooms, but without the spur.

Cultural Information: Columbines are best grown in moisture-retentive but well-drained soil. Space plants 12 to 24 inches apart. They are even more short-lived if they do not have perfect drainage. They self-sow in favorable environments, but offspring of hybrid varieties differ,

Artemisia schmidtiana
'Silver Mound'

*Opposite, from top:
Assorted* Astilbe;
Aster novae-angliae
'Alma Potschke';
Aster x frikartii
*'Wonder of Staffa'
(bottom right); and*
Aster novi-belgii *'Blue
Lake' (bottom left).*

Asclepias tuberosa

sometimes dramatically, from the parent plants. Water generously and use an organic mulch. Sow seeds outdoors in summer or early fall for flowering the following year. Start in sandy flat of soil indoors 12 to 14 weeks before setting out in midspring after danger of frost; refrigerate flat for three weeks, then place in moist, shady place at 70 to 75 degrees Fahrenheit. Do not cover. Germination takes from three to four weeks.
Uses: Border, rock gardens, bedding, background display, cutting, woodland walks, naturalizing.

Artemisia (ar-tay-MIS-ee-a)
mugwort, wormwood, Native American Easy ○ ◗ ☀
Zones: 5 to 8
Height: A. schmidtiana, 6 to 8 inches; *A. ludoviciana,* to 3 feet
Colors: Silvery foliage with small white blooms
Characteristics: Grown for their foliage rather than their inconspicuous flowers with small blooms that open during June and July. Few plants provide foliage texture and color contrast so well as the silver-leafed

artemisias. The finely divided, aromatic foliage that gives the plant a feathery texture is a garden designer's dream and a flower arranger's delight.

Artemisia ludoviciana, 'Silver King', with 3-foot plants, is a quick spreader—use caution where you plant it. *A. schmidtiana,* 'Silver Mound', forms mounds of fernlike foliage, which makes it very useful as garden edging. The clumps are not spreaders and stay much the same size from year to year. Silver plants of all varieties enhance blue perennials.
Cultural Information: Artemisias are not fussy. Any type soil, provided it is well-drained, will suit them. Wet soils, especially during winter, can be fatal. Although they prefer drier soil, moisture is important during the growing season; additional water may be needed during periods of prolonged drought, especially during the first year. If new plants are wanted, make stem cuttings in spring or summer, or divide clumps in spring or fall. Space individual plants 12 to 18 inches apart when planting. Generally pest- and disease-free.
Uses: Edging, border in beds, rock gardens, companion plant, accent.

Asclepias tuberosa (a-SKLAY-pee-as tew-be-RO-sa) **butterfly weed, milkweed** Native American Easy
○ ◗ ▮ ✿
Zones: 4 to 9
Height: 2 to 3 feet
Colors: Orange-red is common but varieties of pale yellow to deep red are available
Characteristics: Butterfly weed

is distinguished by coral buds, which open to brilliant clusters of tiny rose-orange flowers, that bloom in profusion from mid- to late summer—even if not deadheaded. It is very heat- and drought-tolerant, which is why it decorates our roadsides and open woods so luxuriantly. Unlike some roadside plants, butterfly weed is well-behaved in the home garden. One common name comes from the fact that this plant indeed attracts butterflies; the other refers to the milky sap exuded by its stem when cut. If using it as a cut flower, seal the stem by searing with a match. The plant is a wanderer, traveling freely thanks to the seeds attached to silky tufts, easily carried on the wind.
Cultural Information: Butterfly weed prefers well-drained, sandy, or gravelly soils, but will grow in well-prepared clay soils (although the plants tend to freeze in winter if the soil holds too much water). Established plants can withstand drought due to their long taproot. It is this taproot, however, that makes butterfly weed difficult to transplant; it is best left undisturbed. Since these plants sprout late in the spring, mark where you plant them so the buds, which start underground, are not damaged when they emerge.

Seeds germinate in 28 to 42 days, preferring temperatures of 70 to 75 degrees Fahrenheit. Seedlings can be started indoors for bloom the first year, or direct sown outdoors to bloom the following year.
Uses: Cutting, dried, wildflower, middle of the border.

Aster (A-ster) **hardy aster, Michealemas daisy** Native American Easy ○ ◑ 🌡 ✽

Zones: 3 to 8
Height: 18 inches to 5 feet
Colors: White, blue shades, all with gold "orange-yellow" centers
Characteristics: Hardy asters deserve to be used more as they are among the longest blooming and showiest flowers in the late-summer and fall garden. They are not valued for the beauty of their individual blooms, but rather for the mass of color they supply, enlivening the garden at a time when other flowers are scarce. They combine wonderfully with fall-blooming goldenrod, cimicifugas, and chrysanthemums. Fall bouquets are easy because asters are splendid for cutting.

Aster × *frikartii*, 'Wonder of Staffa', is on nearly every expert's list of "Ten Best Perennials." With an exceptional bloom period, from June to November, 18- to 24-inch plants produce a lavish display of ½-inch lavender-blue blooms that few plants can outperform. Try combining with *Coreopsis* 'Early Sunrise', which is its match in long bloom time. *Aster novae-angliae*, the New England aster, has a yellow center with deep purple-blue, narrow petals, a boon to the October garden. 'Harrington's Pink' is a strong, tall (5-foot) variety covered in September and October with shaggy pink buttons that close at night. Loaded with branches and weighed down with flowers, it always needs some stakes.
Cultural Information: Hardy asters are not particular about the soil they grow in, but flower size can be somewhat increased by planting in well-prepared beds. Plant in well-drained soil of average fertility and water frequently, especially during dry weather. In cold climates, asters may require some winter protection (mulch). Pinch back plants in spring and again a month later (before early July) to encourage good branching, and eliminate staking. Bloom season varies with the varieties. With planning it is possible to have different varieties provide continuous bloom from June to November. Deadheading extends bloom period. All asters are easily propagated by division in spring or fall; spring is better in northern climates. Divide every three or four years, discarding the woody center of the crown. Once established, some hardy asters are apt to overrun the garden, becoming more of a pest than a joy. Trespassers should be treated as weeds and the overflow pulled out in the spring.
Uses: Edging, cutting, rock garden, border, woodland walk.

Astilbe (a-STIL-bee) **garden spirea** Easy ◑ ○ 🌡 ✾

Zones: 4 to 8
Height: 12 inches to 3½ feet
Colors: Pink, red, white
Characteristics: Few plants can rival astilbes for grace and charm, with ferny, finely divided foliage sometimes touched with bronze, and feathery flower sprays. Combine with hostas for an easy-care groundcover or border planting.

Astilbe simplicifolia, 'Sprite', has cotton candy pink plumes arching 16 inches above dark-

green, lacy foliage. *A. chinensis* 'Pumila' is only 12 inches high when flowering with soft lavender-pink plumes, a particularly good edger or groundcover. 'Deutschland' sends up 18-inch white plumes that glow in semishady spots or at twilight. There are many varieties from which to choose, and it would be hard to make a bad choice. Plant several different varieties to extend the bloom from early July into September. The plumes are good for cutting and drying.

Cultural Information: Astilbes prefer moist soil supplemented with peat moss or leaf mold. Soil must be well-drained in order for the plants to do well during their winter rest. Astilbes are heavy feeders; feed every spring by mulching with several inches of a good organic mulch or dehydrated cow manure. When dividing, replenish the soil with peat moss, compost, and a dusting of slow-release fertilizer before replanting. Ample water is necessary, especially during dry periods. You can cut back faded flower stalks or let them dry on the plant for added texture in the fall garden. Divide in spring or fall when plants are three to four years old, as they multiply rapidly and exhaust the soil around them.

Uses: Bedding, cutting, companion plant, front of shrubs, groundcover.

Aubrieta (o-bree-AY-ta) **rainbow rock cress** Challenging ○ ◑ ✳ ✿

Zones: 4 to 7
Height: 6 inches
Colors: Deep shades of pink, rose, purple
Characteristics: Aubrietas are very showy, trailing, drooping, spreading plants, sparkling with 1-inch, four-petaled flowers in spring. Their foliage consists of angular, toothed, grayish leaves and is attractive all summer. Blooming April through June—when few perennials bloom—aubrietas are a worthy addition to any garden. Trim back severely after flowering for a second crop to bloom in the summer. Combine them with spring bulbs, which can be planted under an aubrieta groundcover, or in front of bulbs as an edging; they will bloom together, adding contrast, interest, and beauty to your garden. Aubrietas are good companions for their cousins, the *Aurinia*, which bloom at the same time and have a similar habit.
Cultural Information: Aubrietas will grow in light soil but prefer rich, well-drained soils. Good drainage is most important. Water well over long periods of hot, dry weather. Mulch helps to conserve moisture, feed plants, and control weeds. Plants do best where summers are cool. Shear back after flowering to induce more compact habit.

Aubrietas are easily grown from seed, germinating in 14 to 28 days at a temperature of 55 to 65 degrees Fahrenheit; while growing, warmer temperatures are fine. The plants will bloom the following year. No significant pest problems.
Uses: Edging, rock garden, walls and groundcovers.

Aurinia (ow-RIN-ee-a) **basket of gold** Easy ○ ◖ ✳ ◗ ✿

Zones: 4 to 8
Height: 6 to 12 inches
Colors: Lemon to golden yellow
Characteristics: Formerly included in the genus *Alyssum*, aurinias have a draping, sprawling habit, especially suited to rock gardens, hanging baskets, or for growing over the edges of a raised bed. They are charming, dwarf plants that bloom in early spring with narrow, medium-dark to silvery gray-green foliage and clusters of fragrant yellow flowers. Do not confuse with the annual sweet alyssum. Even after flowering, the foliage is attractive in the border and remains throughout the winter. When planted in front of spring-flowering bulbs, aurinias can add fullness, hide bare soil and provide contrast. These reliable, easygoing plants should be grown more often. *A. saxatilis* 'Citrinum' has showers of pale yellow flowers, while *A. saxatilis* 'Compactum' is the plant known as "basket of gold."
Cultural Information: Poor or sandy soil is their preference but they will adapt to any well-drained soil. Limestone in soil is helpful. Aurinias take heat and drought, but water them well during extreme drought. Plant in spring or fall, setting plants 1 to 2 feet apart in all directions. When planting in rock gardens, make sure each plant is given enough room to develop properly. If you are unable to plant nursery plants when purchased, place plants in a cool, shaded area and keep the roots moist. Leggy plants should be cut back after flowering.

Aurinias can be grown from seed, germinating in 21 to 28 days at 60 to 70 degrees Fahrenheit.
Uses: Edging, companion plant, rock garden, hanging baskets, walls, borders.

Baby's breath; see *Gypsophila paniculata*

Baptisia australis (bap-TIS-ee-a ow-STRAH-lis) **false indigo, wild indigo** Native American Easy ○ ◑ ◗

Zones: 3 to 9
Height: 3 to 4 feet
Colors: Blue, white, yellow, violet
Characteristics: Baptisia australis is best known for its indigo-blue flowers and blue-green foliage. This plant is of the pea family (*Leguminosae*) and can grow in low-fertility soil as long as it has sun. It does well in the Deep South, growing wild in the dry, open woods. The 1-inch flowers are pea-shaped, growing along erect spikes. They bloom in late spring and early summer. This plant is long-lived and grows slowly into large clumps the size of small shrubs. Foliage remains dense and lush into the first hard frost. The plant forms long, black seed pods—1½ to 2 inches—at midsummer which can be used in dried flower arrangements. The pods remain on the plant until

Aubrieta

Aurinia saxatilis
'Compactum'

late fall and are an attractive addition to the garden.

Cultural Information: Plant in well-drained soil in full sun or partial shade (this reduces the amount of flowering) about 18 to 24 inches apart. The plant doesn't need to be divided for rejuvenation. It is hard to propagate from division, but if you must divide, do so in early fall or very early spring. It may need staking to prevent breakage. If sown from seed in late fall or early spring, it will flower in two to three years.

Uses: Middle to back of border, cutting, dried arrangements, accent.

Bear's breech; see *Acanthus*

Balloon flower; see *Platycodon*

Basket of gold; see *Aurinia*

Bee balm; see *Monarda*

Bellflower; see *Campanula*

Bergamot; see *Monarda*

Billy buttons; see *Malva*

Black-eyed Susan; see *Rudbeckia*

Blanket flower; see *Gallardia*

Blazing star; see *Liatris*

Bleeding heart; see *Dicentra*

Blue cardinal flower; see *Lobelia*

Blue star; see *Amsonia*

Boltonia (bowl-TOE-nee-a)
Native American Easy
○ ◑
Zones: 3 to 9
Height: 4 to 5 feet
Colors: White
Characteristics: Boltonia asteroides, "Snowbank" is so named because its small silvery foliage with masses of tiny, daisylike clusters look like rather high snowbanks. Boltonias are prolific bloomers, and they provide blooms for cutting from late summer into fall. They are cousins of the Michaelmas asters, and the two are good companion plants when used together. Plant in groups for use in place of shrubs or as landscape accents.

Cultural Information: Ordinary garden soil of medium fertility, or moist, sandy soils, are best for boltonias. They are much more tolerant of extremes of heat and humidity than are asters. They are also vigorous plants, spreading quickly, so plant them in an area with room for growth. They should be lifted and divided for replanting every two to three years, in the fall or spring, or they will become leggy, crowded, and unkempt. If planting of nursery stock is delayed, place plants in a cool, shaded area and keep the roots moist. Set plants 2 to 2½ feet apart when planting.

Uses: Background, accent plant, cutting.

Bugbane; see *Cimicifuga*

Butterfly weed; see *Asclepias tuberosa*

Campanula (kam-PAN-ew-la)
bellflower Easy
○ ◑ ● ✿

Zones: 3 to 7
Height: 1 to 4 feet; *C. carpatica* 6 to 10 inches
Colors: Blue, purple, white
Characteristics: Entire books have been devoted to bellflowers. They come in many sizes, from the tiny *C. carpatica* to the stately cup-and-saucer *C. medium* (the biennial commonly called Canterbury bells). They are mostly in shades of blue and purple with an occasional white variety. The flowers are all bell-shaped, some nodding and some looking up. The shorter varieties tend to be more long-lived than the taller ones. *C. carpatica* has cuplike blue flowers; low-growing and vigorous, reliable, and charming, it has long been a favorite, blooming from June to September. *C. glomerata* has clustered purple-blue, bell-shaped flowers. *C. persicifolia* has erect flowers on short stalks that form a loose cluster rising from a central axis and is a popular cut flower in Europe. *C. rotundifolia,* the bluebells of Scotland, feature nodding, bright blue flowers on slender stems.

Cultural Information: Campanulas are adaptable to any ordinary garden soil but will perform better with richer soils. Provide ample water during blooming period. They prefer a little shade to protect them during the hottest part of the day. Cultivate and mulch to control weeds. All campanulas can be grown from seed one summer to flower the next. They are also easy to propagate by division. The smaller the plants, the more you need to mass them for good garden display. *C. carpatica* should be grouped six or seven

Baptisia australis

Boltonia asteroides 'Snowbank'

Campanula glomerata

Centaurea montana

Centranthus ruber

Cerastium tomentosum
'Silver Carpet'

to a planting, whereas with the larger species *C. persicifolia*, three plants make a good display. For *C. medium* to self-sow, when deadheading leave at least one stalk to go to seed.

Uses: Edger, bedding, rock garden, border, cutting.

Candles of the Lord; see ***Yucca***

Candytuft; see ***Iberis***

Cardinal flower; see ***Lobelia***

Catmint; see ***Nepeta***

Catnip; see ***Nepeta***

Centaurea (sent-OW-ree-a) **knapweed, mountain blue, perennial cornflower** Easy
○ ✳ 🌡

Zones: 4 to 8
Height: 2 to 4 feet
Colors: Blue, purple, yellow, white, pink
Characteristics: Centaureas are perennial members of the daisy family (*Compositae*), which includes the annual cornflower as well as the tender perennial dusty miller. The tufted, long-stemmed flowers bloom mid- to late summer. Some have coarse leaves. *Centaurea montana* is the most popular, with outer florets up to 2½ inches in diameter. *C. dealbata* has unusual leaves that are wooly white underneath, and green and smooth on top; inner florets are red, outer ones are rose to white.

Cultural Information: Centaureas are not fussy about soil as long as it is neither bone dry nor sopping wet. Plant 14 inches apart. They are easily propagated by dividing in early spring. Divide plants every three to four years to keep foliage from becoming dense and crowded. Centaureas spread by underground roots, and it may be necessary to dig up the outside roots yearly if you prefer to contain the plants in a small space. These sturdy plants don't need staking.

Uses: Drying, border, cutting.

Centranthus ruber (sen-TRAN-thus RU-ber) **red valerian, Jupiter's beard** Easy
○ ◑ 🌡 ❀

Zones: 5 to 8
Height: 2 to 4 feet
Colors: Pink, white, shades of red
Characteristics: *Centranthus ruber* is a wildflower in Europe. It is a bushy, floppy plant with 3- to 4-inch gray-green leaves that resemble those of a succulent. The small flowers grow clustered on the stem and their rosy or crimson color is attractive in borders. It is long-blooming, with a great burst in late spring and fewer blooms lasting all summer and into the fall. The cut flowers are long-lasting and can be used for potpourri.

Cultural Information: *C. ruber* needs six hours of sun per day and prefers a dry soil. Sow seed, or propagate by division, in the spring. This plant multiplies rapidly. In England, it is considered a nuisance because it readily self-sows, but

in America it is better behaved, making a good garden plant.

Uses: Border, cutting.

Cerastium (ser-ASS-tee-um) **snow-in-summer** Easy
○ ✳ ❀

Zones: 2 to 9
Height: 4 to 6 inches
Colors: Pure white
Characteristics: Dense, silvery-white foliage is the main attraction of cerastiums, which cover the ground with creeping, trailing, or drooping plants only 4 to 6 inches tall to create the look of a snowfall. They quickly spread and bloom with white, star-shaped flowers in May and June. They are popular plants for crevices of dry walls or rock gardens where they can trail or droop down. 'Silver Carpet' is a recommended variety.

Cultural Information: Cerastiums like lime but will do well in a wide range of soils provided they are well-drained. Shear after flowering to induce bushiness. Cerastiums are very adaptable plants, tolerating even the hot sun on slopes with a southern exposure. The foliage remains all winter but may look unsightly and requires a clean-up of dead leaves in the spring. Sow seeds in spring or late summer for bloom the following year. Can also be propagated by division in spring or fall, or by cuttings of new growth in mid-to late summer.

Uses: Edging, rock garden, groundcover.

Champion; see ***Lychnis***

Chinese lantern; see *Physalis*

Christmas rose; see *Helleborus*

Chrysanthemum

(kris-ANTH-em-um) **Shasta daisy, mums, painted daisy** Difficult
○ ◑ ✳ ◗ ✿

Zones: 5 to 9
Height: 15 to 36 inches
Colors: All colors except blue
Characteristics: Chrysanthemums are America's most popular fall-blooming flowers. However, the genus includes more than 150 species with great variation in appearance and bloom times. The flowers of all species are produced in heads with petallike ray flowers projecting out in single or double forms. The flowers of the fall-blooming chrysanthemums (or mums, as they are often called), also exist in many forms. There are single forms with daisylike flowers; spoon forms have single or semidouble, long tubular petals, flattened at the ends to form a "spoon" that is often a more intense color. The pompon mums are the hardiest and the oldest variety, with dense, full, almost globular flowers. The button pompons are similar, but smaller, the size of a 1-inch button. Quilled varieties are spiky, with petals like quills; they are mostly grown in professional greenhouses. Plan carefully for a succession of blooms and a variety of flower styles.

Chrysanthemum coccineum, better known as the painted daisy, includes large, double and single flowers up to 3 inches across, with rays of white, pink, or rose to dark red projecting from a yellow center. They bloom in June and July, and can be induced to bloom again if cut back after their first bloom. Good, very colorful flowers for bouquets or the garden, they grow 15 to 30 inches high.

C. × superbum is the well-known Shasta daisy. Large, white flowers with single, double, frilled, or fringed petals—all are good cutting flowers. The Shasta daisy is especially showy at twilight and early evening, holding the daylight, reflecting the moonlight. It is easy to grow from seed, sometimes flowering the same season if sown early enough. It needs to be divided every two to three years to keep from crowding. *C. pacificum* is unusual for its neat, attractive foliage, with a velvety white underside that extends to the margin (edges), and when viewed from above gives the leaves a crisp, white edge. It flowers, later than most, in October and well into November, with rayless, bright yellow buttons.

Cultural Information: Chrysanthemums are not fussy about soil, but good drainage is important. To grow them to perfection, spread a few inches of well-rotted or dehydrated cow manure over the soil and incorporate it into the ground to the depth of the spade before planting; feed them with a slow-release plant food several times a year. For bushier, more compact growth, pinch out the tips every few weeks until buds start to form, usually in mid-July. This is a good time to spread a trowelful of dried manure around each plant. You can easily root the pinchings, for a source of additional plants. Chrysanthemums increase rapidly; for better blooms, divide fall-bloomers each spring and summer-bloomers after they bloom, replanting the vigorous growth at the outside of the clumps and discarding the weaker central portions.

Uses: Cutting, corsages, edging, accent among shrubs.

Cimicifuga (sim-i-SIFF-ew-ga)

bugbane, fairy candles Native American Moderately Easy
◑ ◗

Zones: 3 to 8
Height: 3 to 6 feet
Colors: White

Top, left: Cushion Chrysanthemum *'Golden Mound'. Top, right: Quill* Chrysanthemum *'First Lady'. Above: Dwarf* Chrysanthemum maximum.

Spider Chrysanthemum *'Lovely Christine'*

Above: Popular mums.
Below: Chrysanthemum pacificum *'Gold and Silver'.*

Cimicifuga racemosa

Characteristics: These graceful woodland plants send up tall, feathery white jets well above the foliage. Glowing in the dusk, they resemble fairy candles. The elegant spires of tiny white flowers bloom on *C. racemosa* from July through August. This species is admirably suited to woodland plantings or the back of a shady border as a companion plant for monkshood. Plant *C. simplex* 'White Pearl' for late September and October bloom. This species is very showy planted in front of shrubs, and makes for exceptional contrast against the red berries of *Viburnum* species or the reddish-purple fall color of Virginia sweetspire (*Itea virginica*).

Cultural Information: Cimicifugas require moisture-retentive, slightly acid soil, rich in organic matter. To plant bare-root clumps from a division, place rhizome or root stock—with at least two eyes—so that the eyes are 1 inch below soil level. To sow seeds in spring, prechill in the refrigerator for several weeks before planting. Sow at 45 to 50 degrees Fahrenheit. Germination is slow and erratic. The common name, bugbane, may have been given because they are not bothered by insect pests and only rarely by disease.

Uses: Border, woodland walk, shady nook.

Columbine; see *Aquilegia*

Coneflower; see *Echinacea*

Coralbells; see *Heuchera*

Coreopsis (ko-ree-OP-sis) tickseed Native American Easy

○ ◑ ♦ ❀ ❙ ❀
Zones: 3 to 9
Height: 1½ to 3 feet
Colors: Golden yellow
Characteristics: For long bloom and easy care, grow the various species of *Coreopsis*, the happiest and most obliging of perennials. Plants bloom profusely from June to fall. The bright-yellow flowers are exceptionally attractive both in the garden and in arrangements, complemented by dark green, narrow, lobed leaves. *Coreopsis grandiflora* 'Early Sunrise' was bred by Burpee breeder Dennis Flaschenriem and is the only perennial to have won Gold Medals from both All-America Selections and Fleuroselect, its European counterpart; it won for its early bloom (90 to 100 days from sowing) and uniform 24-inch plants that flower from early summer well into fall with golden yellow, semidouble flowers. *C. verticillata* 'Moonbeam' has open, single, daisy-shaped flowers of soft, creamy yellow on compact 1½- to 2-foot plants. The foliage is finely divided and fernlike. 'Moonbeam' blooms faithfully all summer long but is not very heat-tolerant.

Cultural Information: These plants like moist, not soggy, soils with average to rich fertility; they are reasonably drought-tolerant. They may need additional water during periods of prolonged hot, dry weather. Winter mulch of coarse straw, salt hay, or pine branches is needed for protection in colder climates. Keep flowers picked

Above: Coreopsis grandiflora *'Early Sunrise'* ☻.
Below: Coreopsis verticillata *'Moonbeam'.*

to ensure the long blooming period. If planting of nursery stock must be delayed, place plants in a cool, shaded area and keep the roots moist. Space plants 1½ feet apart. Divide after two or three years of blooming. To grow *C. grandiflora* 'Early Sunrise' from seed, start indoors six weeks before the last frost. Seed takes 15 to 20 days to germinate at between 55 and 70 degrees Fahrenheit. Blooms begin eleven weeks from indoor sowing.

Uses: Cutting, middle of the border, containers.

Creeping phlox; see ***Phlox stolonifera***

Daylily; see ***Hemerocallis***

Delphinium (del-FIN-ee-um)
Challenging ○ ◐ ✳ ◊
Zones: 3 to 8
Height: 'Giant Pacific', up to 6 feet; 'Blue Elf', 14 inches; 'Fantasia', 27 inches
Colors: Pink, blue tones, white, with black or white "bees" (centers)
Characteristics: These beautiful plants can be the glory of a June garden. They are unequalled for contributing elegance to the border, their tall spires lined with flat, single-, or double-rosette blooms that contrast with the dark green, broad to finely cut leaves.

D. elatum 'Giant Pacific' is the great big fellow that draws raves. Majestic plants grow up to 6 feet tall, with 5-foot spikes, and florets that are often marked with contrasting centers, or "bees."

Burpee-bred, *D. elatum* 'Fantasia' is easy to grow from seed, blooming the first season if started early enough. 'Fantasia' is a semidwarf plant only 27 inches high, with flower spikes as large and showy as tall delphiniums, but it needs no staking. A good color mixture of white, lavender, and shades of blue, all accented with creamy white bees. *D. grandiflorum* 'Blue Elf', a compact, 14-inch plant with very finely divided foliage, has intense mid-blue florets on graceful spikes that bloom all summer. The foliage of all delphiniums is poisonous if eaten.

Cultural Information: Light, deeply worked soil with good drainage and enriched with compost is necessary to grow delphiniums. The plants are heavy feeders and appreciate being fertilized several times throughout the season with a slow-release 5–10–5 fertilizer. Slightly alkaline soil is best, and very acid soil should be limed for them. Keep established plants well-watered, but soil should not be soggy. They thrive on cool, moist summer nights. Only under these soil and weather conditions will delphiniums be a permanent addition to your plantings. Where conditions are less than ideal, they tend to be short-lived; in that case, plant them as annuals. Cultivate and mulch to control weeds. Winter mulch may be needed for cooler areas, applied after the ground has frozen. Plant in spring, after danger of frost, 1½ to 3 feet apart. Tall varieties will require staking for support. Many gardeners prefer to tie string between two or three stakes, giving each plant room to move

with the breeze within the stake "corral." After the first blush of bloom in June is over, cut back and they may bloom again in fall. They need dividing after three years of flowering. In the early spring, as shoots are breaking through the ground, carefully dig up clumps; wash soil away and cut clumps into sections with a sharp knife. Each section should have one strong stem and plenty of fibrous roots. All new clumps should be planted immediately in well-prepared, enriched soil.

Uses: Back of the border, cutting.

Dianthus (dy-ANTH-us) **pinks**
Moderately Easy ○ ◊ ❀
Zones: 3 to 8
Height: 10 to 18 inches; *D. barbatus*, 6 inches to 2 feet
Colors: Rose, pink, red, white, salmon, yellow
Characteristics: Outstanding, spicy fragrance and evergreen tufts of silver, blue, or green foliage have endeared these plants to gardeners for centuries. They grow best in full sun, producing dozens of long-lasting blooms from May through June. 'Helen' is an exceptionally free bloomer, bearing scores of rich salmon pink flowers on strong, 10- to 12-inch stems. Blooms early summer into fall if picked frequently.

D. barbatus is the old-fashioned sweet William, a biennial that, if happy, will reseed. The species comes in a variety of colors and bicolors from 6 inches to 2 feet in height. These are among the showiest members of the genus.

D. chinensis is a fragrant, old-fashioned fringed pink popular for growing along garden paths.

Delphinium *'Fantasia'*

Dianthus *'Spring Beauty'*

Dianthus *'Helen'*

Dicentra spectabilis

Dicentra spectabilis
'*Alba*'

Dictamnus albus
purpureus

It needs excellent drainage and is likely to die if grown where water can sit in puddles.

Cultural Information: Pinks prefer very well-drained, sandy or gritty soil. Add lime to very acid soil, but don't fertilize; pinks prefer poorer, less fertile soil. Do not mulch, as this encourages rot. If you use the plants as edgers, space them 8 to 12 inches apart. Plant in fall or late spring, after danger of frost; spring is safer in areas where winters are severe. If nursery plantings must be delayed, place plants in a cool, shaded area and keep the roots moist. Plants usually lose vigor after the second year of blooming and should be divided or replaced. They can be easily grown from seed or from cuttings. Cuttings should be moved to their permanent place in the garden when young, before their long and rangy roots get big. The flowers are long-lasting when cut but the fragrance fades after a day or two.

Uses: Edging, front of the border, rock garden.

Dicentra (dy-SEN-tra) **bleeding heart** Native American Moderately Easy

◗ ● ○ ✳ ▮ ❀

Zones: 3 to 9
Height: 1 to 2½ feet; dwarf, 10 to 30 inches
Colors: Pink, red, white
Characteristics: The swiftly passing splendor of the old-fashioned bleeding heart (*D. spectabilis*) is probably why dicentras are not found as frequently in today's gardens. The attractive, ornamental foliage will remain in good condition all summer,

provided the plants are not allowed to dry out. Particularly at home in the woodland garden, dicentras boast graceful, compound leaves and bear arching stems of pendant, heart-shaped flowers in spring. Especially beautiful in the midst of late-season tulips, they lend an airiness to spring gardens. They go dormant and die back to their roots late in summer, to emerge once again in all their glory the following year.

The fringed bleeding heart (*D. eximia*) is dwarf—10 to 12 inches—and flowers off and on all summer. It makes a soft groundcover and provides flowers for cutting all summer.

Cultural Information: Dicentras like humus-rich, well-drained soil in partial shade. Plant early fall or early spring and leave undisturbed. Water and feed regularly, but cut back when the dormant period begins. Because they last for years, dicentras tend to become overcrowded and need dividing in three to four years. Dig them up in early spring and handle the roots very carefully because they are extremely brittle. Each piece of root division should have an eye, but the root need not be more than 3 inches long. New planting locations should be well-marked to protect any early growth or dormant roots from cultivation accidents. For continuous blooming all summer of *D. eximia*, remove the spent blossoms regularly. It is easiest to purchase young plants from the nursery or catalogs before new growth begins in spring. Space plants 2 feet apart; space rows 3 feet apart. They can be started from seed but require a lot of patience. Sow

seeds in late fall or early winter outdoors or indoors in small flats, freezing for six weeks. Move to a warm place at 55 to 60 degrees Fahrenheit, where they will germinate; seedlings appear in three to five weeks.

Uses: Borders, rock gardens, woodland walks, groundcovers, cutting.

Dictamnus albus (dik-TAM-nus AL-bus) **gas plant** Moderate

○ ◑ ● ❀

Zones: 3 to 8
Height: 3 feet
Colors: White, salmon pink streaked with violet
Characteristics: Once established, members of the genus *Dictamnus* are long-lasting and worth waiting for, some of the most permanent of the hardy perennials. They are very slow-growing, taking three years to flower and longer to become a bushy, established clump. But once established, they provide showy, spiky flowers from June through July. Their glossy, clean, fragrant foliage stays attractive until frost. The common name, gas plant, is derived from the fact that the plant gives off a volatile oil that can sometimes actually be ignited in the evening without damage to the plant. The flowers are not good for cutting, but the seed pods are attractive in dried arrangements.

Cultural Information: Plant in a well-drained, heavy soil high in organic matter, in full sun or light shade. Allow 3 feet on all sides, as these plants become bushy. They do not like to be disturbed, so division is sometimes unsuccessful. When well-rooted, they can withstand drought and neglect and should be allowed to remain undisturbed for years, as the flowers improve with age. Young nursery plants transferred to the garden in the spring are the most common way to start this plant. To start from seed, sow outdoors in late fall, early winter. They will germinate the next spring but will do better if you wait until the following spring to transplant. Seedlings do not take well to transplanting, so plant in individual peat pots. These bushy plants do not need staking.

Uses: Border.

Digitalis (di-ji-TAH-lis) **foxglove** Easy ◑ ○ ▮ ✿

Zones: 4 to 9
Height: 3 feet
Colors: Purple, pink, white, red, yellow and bicolors
Characteristics: Lovely at the rear of the border or on a woodland walk, foxgloves bloom with tall spikes of bell-shaped flowers in late spring and early summer. The light green leaves form a low rosette, evergreen in all but the coldest climates. Most foxgloves, however, are not perennial, but biennial, and establish large clumps because they self-sow freely. *Digitalis* × *mertonensis* is a truly perennial foxglove, bearing spikes of bell-shaped flowers the color of strawberry ice cream. *D. purpurea* 'Excelsior' is a biennial with superior, large flowers borne horizontally all around the stem rather than the usual pendant blooms on all three sides. 'Foxy' is the only foxglove that will bloom from seed the first year, approximately five months after sowing.

Cultural Information: Foxgloves are best grown in well-drained yet moisture-retentive soil, rich in leaf mold or other organic matter. Space 1 foot apart. Plant nursery plants in the spring or fall. Sow seed outdoors in late spring or early summer for flowers the following spring. They can be started indoors at 70 degrees Fahrenheit and will germinate in one to three weeks. Taller varieties will probably need staking. If the flower stalks are cut back after flowering, they might bloom again in the fall. If you want the plant to reseed, leave at least one stalk standing. Protect with salt hay or other winter mulch in northern climates. Foliage is poisonous if eaten.

Uses: Back of the border, woodland walk.

Double bouncing bet; see *Saponaria*

Echinacea (e-kee-NAH-see-a) **coneflower** Native American Easy ○ ◑ ▮ ✳ ▮ ✿

Zones: 3 to 9
Height: 2 to 5 feet
Colors: Reddish purple, white
Characteristics: The daisylike petals bend back to expose a stiff, quill-like, golden crimson cone in the center. The shape and movement of echinaceas are reminiscent of the shuttlecocks of badminton as they float gracefully in the breeze.

Echinaceas are native to open woodlands and prairies from Georgia to Louisiana, Iowa and Ohio, where they thrive and tolerate drought. The plants have bold foliage, rough, hairy stems, and somewhat oval, 5- to 9-inch

long leaves. The flowers are 3 to 4 inches across, and the central cone is higher, with the petals drooping. Both the blooms and the attractive seed heads that follow them are excellent for arrangements. These are long-blooming flowers from July into September. 'Ovation' is a worthy, rosy pink variety, and 'White Swan' is a reliable white.

Cultural Information: Echinaceas grow in a wide range of soils, from sandy to rich, but always need good drainage. Never allow them to grow in soggy soils, especially during the winter. These plants are drought-resistant, but initial plantings should be well-watered. During long periods of hot, dry weather during the season of growth, supply plants with additional water. Remove faded blooms to keep plants neat and encourage new bloom. In cold climates, a light winter covering of salt hay or evergreen branches is appreciated. Apply this protection after the soil has frozen. Plants may be left undisturbed for years. To prevent overcrowding, divide clumps after three years of flowering. Space plants 18 inches apart. The strong stems rarely need staking. Can easily be grown from seed planted in the fall to bloom the following summer.

Uses: Cutting, border, background plants.

Echinops (EK-in-ops) **globe thistle** Moderate ○ ▮ ✿

Zones: 3 to 8
Height: 4 to 5 feet
Colors: Violet to steel blue
Characteristics: The spiky steel-blue balls of echinops lend

Digitalis purpurea

Echinacea purpurea

Echinops *'Ritro'*

Eupatorium coelestinum *and* Eupatorium rugosum

Gaillardia grandiflora *'Dazzler'*

subtle color and interesting texture with prickly foliage for several weeks at the rear of the border. Their blue color gradually changes to silver. They are beautiful when combined with pink perennial phlox or white Japanese anemones. These plants offer outstanding long-lasting flowers—and foliage—for fresh or dried arrangements. They bloom July through August, sometimes into September. *Cultural Information:* Echinops grow best in well-drained soil of average fertility. Space plants 18 to 24 inches apart. They can be difficult to divide, as roots are about 1 foot deep and dense. It is necessary to divide every three to four years in the early spring. Some gardeners report rashes from repeated rubbing against the foliage, so care should be taken. The foliage at the bottom of the plants is sometimes tattered; this is best concealed by growing smaller plants in front.
Uses: Cutting, dried, border.

Eupatorium (yew-pa-TO-ree-um) **Joe-Pye weed, hardy ageratum, mist flower** Native American Easy ○ ◐ ▮ ✿
Zones: 5 to 9
Height: *E. coelestinum* 'Gateway', 1 to 3 feet; *E. purpureum*, 4 to 6 feet
Colors: Purplish pink, white
Characteristics: Eupatoriums, with their dome-shaped clusters of flowers atop deep red stems, bloom in late summer and fall. They do extremely well at the boggy ends of ponds, meadows, or streams. They make magnificent accent plants, and combine well with tall ornamental grasses. They can also be used as natural decorations (less formal) for the corners of a garden.

This American native is more popular with breeders in Europe. 'Gateway' is a new selection, better behaved than its roadside cousins, which tend to be taller and floppier, with fewer flowers. Flowers can be cut before fully opened and hung upside down in a dark, well-ventilated place to dry.
Cultural Information: Plant eupatoriums in rich, moist soil in spring or fall. Turn the soil well and incorporate compost or peat moss to help hold moisture. Water regularly for the first year to help the plants become better established. They are easily grown and perfectly hardy, but because they do not appear in spring until most plants have pushed their heads well above the soil, eupatoriums are often thought to be dead. Many gardeners accidentally cut the plants' roots to pieces in spring. It is therefore advisable to put a row of stakes around the plants in the fall before they die down, as a reminder when spring comes. Mulch the soil around individual plants with compost, shredded leaves, or lawn cuttings. Plants can be divided after they flower or when the clumps begin to dwindle from overcrowding.
Uses: Corners of the garden, borders, cutting, meadows, open woodlands.

Evening primrose; see *Oenothera*

Fairy candles; see *Cimicifuga*

False dragonhead; see *Physostegia*

False indigo; see *Baptisia*

Fleur de Lis; see *Iris*

Foxglove; see *Digitalis*

Funkia; see *Hosta*

Gaillardia
(gay-LARD-ee-a) **blanket flower** Native American Easy ○ ▮ ✳ ▮ ✿
Zones: 3 to 9
Height: 6 inches to 3 feet
Colors: Yellow with maroon centers
Characteristics: For hot, vivid color in your garden and lots of cheerful cut flowers, plant gaillardias. Their foliage is rough, hairy, green, and lance-shaped. Gaillardias are part of our American horticultural heritage and indigenous to the hills, plains, and prairies of the West, where they survive drought, blooming freely virtually all summer. They have adapted beautifully to cultivated gardens where their bright, daisy flowers are borne profusely from June to frost.

'Dazzler' is a 2-foot variety covered with golden yellow flowers with fiery red centers.
Cultural Information: Gaillardias must have well-drained soil. They are valuable plants where heat and drought are problems. Remove faded blooms regularly for further flowering. The plants often need staking. Divide plants when they become overcrowded, after two to three years of flowering. Seeds can be sown in

spring or root cuttings taken in summer for bloom the following year. Plant in spring 10 to 12 inches apart.
Uses: Background, cutting, dried.

Garden phlox; see *Phlox paniculata*

Garden spirea; see *Astilbe*

Gas plant; see *Dictamnus*

Gaura lindheimeri

(GAW-ra lind-HY-mer-i) Native American Easy

○ ◐ ✳ ▮ ❀

Zones: 6 to 9
Height: 3 to 4 feet
Colors: Pinkish white flowers
Characteristics: Flowers resembling white butterflies appear throughout the summer along the stems. Each fine stem carries just a few delicate leaves, but there are many stems in each plant and together they form clumps of graceful, bushy plants. Gauras are long-flowering —early summer to first frost— but they can get leggy and floppy. A good pruning in midsummer will correct this and bring more flowers. Where summers are cool, plants will not flower until late summer. Planting among or behind stiffer perennials will help hold their floppy stems up.
Cultural Information: Plant gauras in deep, sandy soil enriched with compost and raise the bed if necessary to ensure that water drains rapidly. Watering is needed only after prolonged drought. Plants are easily raised from seed or propagated from cuttings taken in the summer. Space plants 18 inches apart

to allow them room to grow. Clumps rarely need dividing. To move, use a spade and dig deep carefully to avoid damaging the root.
Uses: Cutting, back of border.

Gayfeather; see *Liatris*

Globeflower; see *Trollius*

Globe thistle; see *Echinops*

Ground pinks; see *Phlox subulata*

Ground phlox; see *Phlox subulata*

Gypsophila paniculata

(jip-SOF-i-la pan-ik-ew-LAH-ta)
baby's breath Moderate

○ ▮ ❀

Zones: 3 to 10
Heights: 3 to 4 feet; dwarf, 18 inches
Colors: White
Characteristics: Clouds of airy flowers cover *G. paniculata* all summer if the plant is sheared after the blooms fade. The plant is branched, having wiry stems with grasslike foliage of a medium green to gray-green color. The blooms lighten the effect of denser plants in the garden and are an excellent follow-up to poppies; they will grow and fill in the garden while the poppies are dying back. For dried bouquets, flowers are picked when fully open and hung upside down by their stems in a dark, dry, well-ventilated place. 'Early Snowball' grows to 3 feet and is covered with mostly double flowers of pearly white. 'Viette's Dwarf Form' is a compact variety only 18

inches tall and requiring no staking.
Cultural Information: Grow *G. paniculata* in rich, deep soil that is well-drained. Although sometimes called "chalk plant" and tolerant of lime, it does not require an alkaline soil to prosper. It will become quite bushy, so allow 3 feet between each plant. In very acid soil, spread lime around the plant stems once per year (but do not let it come into direct contact with roots). To prolong bloom, keep flowers sheared before they set seed. *G. paniculata* is difficult to divide owing to its fleshy taproot system; division is not recommended—but if you must do it, do it in the spring. In Zones 4 and 5, the plant should be protected with a straw or salt hay mulch after the ground freezes. Mulch should be removed in the spring before new growth appears. Easily sown from seed outdoors in spring or early summer, or indoors in spring. The plant needs to be supported at the base to help it hold a full, round shape: Surround the plant with four to six 1-foot stakes. Weave string (green is best) in and out around the stakes several times. The

Gaura lindheimeri

Gypsophila 'Viette's Dwarf Form'

plant will grow up through the string and flop back down over the top, to form a ball of tiny, white flowers.

Uses: Drying, filler in bouquets, borders.

Hardy ageratum; see *Eupatorium*

Hardy aster; see *Aster*

Helleborus (he-LE-bo-rus) **hellebore, Lenten rose, Christmas rose** Moderate
◑ ✳ ❚ ❀

Zones: 4 to 9, depending on variety
Height: 1 to 3 feet
Colors: White flushed with pink, green, pink, purple
Characteristics: Hellebores bloom in midwinter, cheering us when almost everything else is asleep in northern gardens. What a delight to be greeted by the drooping, buttercup flowers of hellebores. The Christmas rose (*H. niger*) blooms first with cream or greenish cream flowers that fade to brownish yellow or purple-brown. Their cup-shaped flowers, up to 2½ inches across,

Helleborus foetidus

Helleborus niger

hold yellow stamens and sometimes are speckled with purple. They open with the snowdrops but continue blooming for weeks longer. The flowers are practically hidden by the large foliage early in the season but are easier to see later when they rise above it. Plant them where you can view them up close. The foliage is evergreen; it suffers from the ravages of winter but replaces itself in the spring. Later the Lenten rose (*H. orientalis*) blooms with white or pink-tinged flowers.

Cultural Information: Plant hellebores in humus-rich soil before frost. They seldom need dividing. The plants resent transplanting and should be placed in their permanent place young. At temperatures below 15 degrees Fahrenheit, bloom is delayed and, unless snow-protected, the evergreen leaves can become damaged. Because it blooms so early, *H. niger* is best planted where it can be protected from the ravages of winter. The roots are poisonous. Growing from seed isn't difficult but it is slow. Occasionally, plants will self-sow; check around the base of the plants in the spring for seedlings that can be moved, protected, and grown on in pots, to be returned to a new spot in the garden next year.

Uses: Woodland walk, border, shady garden.

Hemerocallis (hay-me-ro-KA-lis) **daylily** Easy
○ ◑ ◗ ✺ ❀

Zones: 3 to 10
Height: 5 feet; dwarf, 18 inches
Colors: Yellow, orange, red, pink, purple, melon, lavender

Characteristics: A perfect bloom one day, gone the next: This is the fleeting cycle of flowering daylilies. Waiting in the wings is another flower, and yet another, continuing the bloom of each plant for several weeks. Daylilies are very nearly the perfect perennials. They're easy to grow, trouble-free, need little maintenance, and thrive under unfavorable conditions. The varieties available today are a far cry from the familiar tawny orange daylilies that naturalized along roadsides many years ago in the eastern states. Now these trumpet flowers are larger, some up to 9 inches diameter, with double, ruffled or twisted petals. They bloom over a longer period, and the color range has been expanded to include melon, pink, red, lavender, and purple, in addition to the familiar yellow and orange. Many attractive bicolors are available now. Look for fragrant species like the lemon lily (*H. lilioasphodelus*). One of the most exceptional cultivars is *H.* × *hybrida* 'Stella de Oro', a dwarf (18-inch) variety whose yellow flowers bloom continuously for three months; its compact size means it can be grown in a container.

Prime season for daylilies is June and July in most of the United States, but by choosing varieties that bloom in succession, you can have blooms into September. Mass daylilies wherever you need a colorful, care-free landscape accent. In a few years, the long, arching fountainlike foliage fills in and provides cascades of willowy green dancers in the summer breeze, handsome enough even when not in flower to provide a backdrop for other flowers, and dense enough to keep weeds from growing. Southern gardens can grow the evergreen types. Since there are more than thirty thousand names for daylily cultivars, have a wonderful time choosing!

Cultural Information: Daylilies grow almost anywhere, but they do best in a minimum of six hours of sun, in a moisture-retentive soil. Plant them 2 feet apart (or closer, if you're impatient for an established bed). They multiply generously but stay neat and are not invasive. If new, bare-rooted plants arrive or if you divide plants and can't replant immediately, don't let them dry out. They will be fine in a bucket with a little water in the bottom, placed in a cool spot for a few days, if the water is changed daily. When they start to crowd, after three or four years, dig up the roots in spring or fall and divide. Each division should have one fan of leaves. Mulch in summer to conserve moisture. Fertilize with a slow-release 12–12–12 fertilizer, lightly once

each spring, and repeat applications during summer and fall. Make sure they are well-watered weekly, early in the season, as drought retards the formation of flower buds. In light shade, the production of flowers may be less satisfactory than in full sun, but you'll enjoy the foliage all season.

Uses: Cutting, border, accent plant, holding a bank.

Heuchera (hew-KER-a)

coralbells Native American
Easy ○ ◑ ❗ ✿
Zones: 4 to 8
Height: 1 to 2 feet
Colors: White, pink, red
Characteristics: Coralbells are perennials with many attributes. The common name most fittingly describes the flower color and shape. One of the plant's best features is its ability to do well almost anywhere. Plants mature in about one year with attractive evergreen, ivy-shaped leaves and slender wandlike stems that carry tiny bell flowers in early summer (sometimes off and on again throughout the summer). The bright green or deep bronze foliage forms attractive basal

Top: Hemerocallis *'Pompian Rose'*. *Center:* Hemerocallis *'Hypericum'*. *Above:* Dwarf Hemerocallis *'Stella de Oro'*. *Left:* Heuchera *'Palace Purple'*.

clumps. Flower arrangers find their long-lasting blooms good for cutting and excellent subjects for drying. Coralbells are native to California, New Mexico, Arizona, and south into Mexico. *Heuchera americana* 'Dale's Selection' is a striking native, particularly at home on dry banks and tolerant of even infertile soils. Handsomely scalloped, purple-blue leaves with deep blue veins provide all-season display, enhanced in June and July by delicate sprays of white flowers tinged with green. The 'Bressingham' hybrids of *H. sanguinea* have green foliage and flowers in shades of pink, white, and deep rose.

Cultural Information: Plant coralbells in spring in well-drained soil with ample humus. Set crowns 1 inch below the soil level. In spring, remove any damaged leaves to prevent them from rotting on the plant and spreading disease. As flowers fade, remove them to encourage later bloom. In severely cold areas, it is necessary to apply a mulch to ensure survival over winter; salt hay or any light material that does not pack down

Hosta 'Honey Bells'

Hosta variegata

should prove satisfactory. Divide plants in spring when they become overcrowded, usually after four to five years of flowering. New plants are easy to start from leaf cuttings made in late fall. Each cutting needs a short section of leafstalk, in addition to an entire leaf, to root in sand (see propagating by cuttings, page 32). Sow seeds outdoors in spring and they will produce flowers the following year. Do not cover seed after pressing into the soil, as they need light to germinate. Sow seeds indoors in late winter or early spring, optimally at 50 to 60 degrees Fahrenheit. Seeds germinate in about twenty days. There must be excellent drainage to avoid crown rot, especially in winter. Stems also may rot in heavy, wet soils and humid climates. If foliage rots in summer after heavy rains, cut it away to prevent the spread of disease.

Uses: Cutting, drying, front of border, groundcover.

Hollyhock; see *Alcea*

Honesty plant; see *Lunaria*

Horned violet; see *Viola*

Hosta (HOS-ta) **funkia, plantain lily** Easy ◐ ● ⬛

Zones: 3 to 9
Height: 18 inches to 3 feet
Colors: Pale lilac to white flowers
Characteristics: Hostas are popular, indispensable plants for a shady garden. They are easy to grow, long-lived, and virtually carefree, naturalizing in moderately rich, partly shaded

places. Best of all, hostas quickly spread into dense, ground-hugging clumps that thwart weeds. Hostas are equally at home in a woodland setting, formally lined against a north-facing brick wall, or providing an accent in the flower border. They are unsurpassed as a groundcover, with many choices of foliage from various shades of green, to variegated blue-green or gold. All varieties produce lovely flowers in summer, often fragrant, on long, graceful stems. The flowers are exceptionally long-lasting and attractive in arrangements. Individual flowers are shaped like small lilies, 1½ inches long on short, erect stems that form in clusters of eight to ten blossoms.

Hostas range in size. 'Frances Williams' is one of the largest, forming clumps with 1- to 2-foot blue-tinged, puckered leaves edged with creamy yellow bands. 'Francee' has dark green, heart-shaped leaves with sparkling white margins and spikes of lavender flowers. The leaves of 'Gold Standard' form clumps 18 inches high and turn from light green to gold, edged in dark green by summer. 'Krossa Regal' has a different look, with large, smooth, frosty blue leaves that stand up like tall vases.

Cultural Information: Grown in full or partial shade, hostas need well-drained soil high in organic matter. Avoid wet, soggy soils, which will cause them to rot. Full sun in hot climates will burn the foliage. They need regular, deep watering during dry spells. Mulching in winter may help young plants started in fall survive a tough winter, but it is not necessary as a rule. Hostas are unusual in that they never require division, but are easy to divide and transplant if you want to increase their numbers. To propagate, divide plants under three years old in spring or early fall. Slugs love hostas, so keep a watchful eye.

Uses: Groundcover, accent of flower border, woodland walk, cutting.

Hybrid anemone; see *Anemone × hybrida*

Iberis sempervirens

(eye-BEER-is sem-per-VI-renz) **candytuft** Easy ○ ◗ ✳

Zones: 4 to 8
Height: 16 inches
Colors: White
Characteristics: This is one of the best, low-growing evergreen perennials for early spring. It is almost completely covered with clusters of white flowers, many lasting into early summer. The foliage is shrublike, dark green, and has narrow leaves 1 to 2 inches long. The plant is attractive throughout the year with its matlike habit and dwarf size.

Cultural Information: Space plants 6 to 12 inches apart in light, sandy soil that is well-drained and slightly acidic. They can be planted in early fall or late spring, after all danger of frost. They will need to be watered during a drought. Shear plants back severely after blooming to keep them neat. If flowers are continually picked after blooming, it will prolong the blooming period. The plants

should be left undivided as long as they flower well. Propagate from seed or make cuttings in late summer, then winter them over in a cold frame where they can be kept moist and protected from the elements.

Uses: Edger, rock gardens, groundcover.

Iris (EYE-ris) Easy
○ ◗

Zones: 3 to 9
Height: 6 inches to 4 feet; dwarf, 4 to 6 inches
Colors: All colors
Characteristics: There is more to the genus *Iris* than the most popular iris variety, the tall, bearded "German" iris that blooms in May or June. There is great diversity in size, bloom time, and flower form, from the miniature, 6-inch, native American *I. cristata*, crested iris, with its delicate, light lavender flower crested with orange, to the 30-inch Japanese native *I. kaempferi* that boasts a flat head, sometimes 10 inches across.

Irises are favorites all over the world. Consequently, in addition to the best-known German irises, we have (to name a few) English, Spanish, Dutch, Persian, California, Japanese, and Siberian irises. The only problem with the taller irises is that the bloom season always seems too brief. For diversity try some of these:

I. cristata: An American wildflower 6 inches high that can be planted as a groundcover with its vigorous compact growth. Once established, it keeps weeds out. Grow in Zones 3 to 9 for flowering late spring.

Hosta 'Krossa Regal'

Above: Hosta fortunei 'Aureo-marginata'.
Right: Iberis sempervirens 'Purity'.

Iris reticulata

Iris sibirica

Iris germanica 'Gay Parade'

Iris germanica 'Raspberry Blush'

Iris danfordiae: These dwarf, 4- to 6-inch harbingers of spring should be planted where they can be viewed up close. I have a large clump that allows me to pick some to brighten February days indoors. Grows well in Zones 5 to 9.

Iris reticulata: This is one of the earliest blooming (sometimes in later winter, usually early spring), with 6-inch-high stems, and royal purple and gold flowers. The bulbs need to be buried 2 to 3 inches deep and grouped by the dozens to put on a show. They disappear by late spring and can be overplanted with annuals.

Iris germanica: The German irises that hybridization has made available in a breathtaking array of colors and bicolors bear little resemblance to their rather austere ancestors. They require very well-drained soil. These are the bearded irises with upright petals called "standards," the lower drooping petals are "falls," and located on the upper part of the falls are furry tufts or "beards." Grow in full sun in Zones 3 to 10.

Iris sibirica, Siberian iris: bloom atop 2- to 3-foot stems rising from clumps of attractive, grassy foliage after the German irises have finished. Grow in full sun in Zones 3 to 9.

Iris kaempferi: The Japanese irises have large, flat flowers with ornate patterns of vining in contrasting colors. They hold their flat faces to the sky. Their foliage is long and flat, arching in grassy clumps that are attractive in the border even when the plant isn't flowering. The Japanese have, over centuries, developed these irises by eliminating the standards and increasing the size of the falls. They prefer acidic, organic-rich soil with constant moisture. Grow in sun or part shade in Zones 4 to 9.

Cultural Information: Different species have different requirements. Some like their feet constantly wet, some like them moist and others seemingly are indifferent. Irises are classified as bulbous or rhizomatous. The bulbous group contains *I. reticulata* and other small, early varieties that need to be treated more like crocuses. Plant several inches deep, with the foliage allowed to ripen and die back before being removed in the spring.

Most irises have rhizomes, horizontally creeping stems which must be shallowly planted with the top of the rhizome exposed.

A well-drained soil is necessary for all irises. Avoid the use of fresh manures around the plants, but well-rotted compost, worked in at least 12 inches deep, can be beneficial. A neutral soil pH is best for most irises; the Siberian and Japanese types are exceptions, preferring a slightly acid soil. In early spring, when foliage appears, apply a side dressing of high-phosphorus fertilizer (avoid putting any directly over the rhizomes).

It is important to keep weeds cleaned up, especially any grass that might grow around the rhizomes. Clean cultivation should prevent any troublesome problems from getting a head start. In spring or fall, check to be sure that rhizome tops are even with the soil surface. When planting new rhizomes, spread out the roots and carefully firm the soil around their sides. If soil is heavy, do not cover the top third of the rhizomes; if light or slightly sandy, some covering will not be harmful. Space plants 12 to 18 inches apart. All new planting should be well-watered. Keep soil moist, but not wet, around established plantings. In the fall, cut foliage back 1 to 2 inches above the ground level and destroy all cuttings. It is always best to remove faded flowers, in order to keep the plants in top growing condition and prevent rot and disease. Bearded irises multiply quickly and should be dug up and divided the third or fourth year of flowering. After flowers fade, dig up the clump with a spading fork and clip the leaves to a length of 4 to 6 inches. Cut off fleshy outer portions of the rhizomes with a sharp knife, dividing them into pieces with at least two fans of leaf per section. Discard the central parts of the rhizomes and replant the good sections immediately. It is important to destroy all dead foliage in the fall because it carries disease spores and insect eggs. Winter protection (mulch) is needed only in the most severe winters, when plants are exposed without snow cover. A loose mulch of coarse straw may be an advantage, provided it does not mat down and keep rhizomes wet. Mulches offer a cover for mice, which can destroy the rhizomes.

Uses: Border, edge of a stream or pond, cutting, groundcover.

Italian alkanet, Italian Bugloss; see *Anchusa*

Japanese anemone; see *Anemone ×hybrida*

Joe-pye weed; see *Eupatorium*

Jupiter's beard; see *Centranthus*

Knapweed; see *Centaurea*

Kniphofia uvaria (nee-FOF-ee-a oo-VAH-ree-a) **red-hot poker, torch lily** Moderate ○ 🌡

Zones: 6 to 9
Height: 2 to 4 feet, some up to 6 feet
Colors: Flaming red, red-orange blending into yellow; some solids in ivory, yellows, corals
Characteristics: This torchlike lily produces graceful, arching mounds of grasslike leaves and erect spikes of brilliant flowers that create an exotic and tropical effect in any garden. An African plant, it is not reliably hardy in northern gardens and will require some protection, but it is hardy south of Philadelphia. It is best left undisturbed for years. The species bloom in August and September, while the hybrids bloom in June, July, or August. The foliage forms dense, tufted mounds 12 to 20 inches in height, from which arise stiff "pokers" which reach 2 to 4 feet tall. Most blooming coincides with daylilies and makes a good contrast. Where they flower early, they often repeat bloom in the fall.

Cultural Information: Set plants at least 1½ to 2 feet apart in moderately fertile, moist (well-drained), sandy loam in spring or fall. Spring plantings are safer where winters are severe. They are difficult to stake attractively, so avoid windy areas and they will be self-sufficient. Mulch over the winter in areas where temperatures drop below 0 degrees Fahrenheit. In severe climates, it would be considered best to lift the plants in the fall, storing the roots in dry sand in a warm—not hot—place. Divide every four to five years, in spring only. You may divide all the roots or simply dig up offsets, which form on the side of the main crown. Make sure these have roots, then replant.

Uses: In front of shrubs, cutting, back of border.

Lamb's ear; see *Stachys byzantia*

Lenten rose; see *Helleborus*

Liatris (lee-AHT-ris) **gayfeather, blazing star** Native American Easy ○ 🌡

Zones: 3 to 9
Height: 2 to 6 feet
Colors: Pinkish lavender, purple, white, rose
Characteristics: Gayfeathers are showy plants, ideal for the border, fine by the waterside, and useful for cutting. The wand-like, stiff flower stalks grow from 3 to 5 feet long and are made up of individual fuzzy florets. The plants are quite unusual in that the flower spikes usually begin to open at the top of the spike first, rather than in the normal bottom-to-top sequence of other spiky plants such as snapdragons. Butterflies and bees are attracted to the flowers. The plants form thick clumps of basal foliage, above which rise flower spikes in midsummer. Cutting back spent flower spikes will extend the bloom. Some good garden varieties include *L. scariosa* 'White Spires', a 3-foot, white variety, *L. spicata* 'Kobold', a 2-foot, dark purple variety, and *L. pycnostachys* 'Kansas Gayfeather', a tall variety (up to 6 feet) available in white or purple.

Cultural Information: Set plants in well-drained average soil. To prevent overcrowding, divide clumps after three to four years of flowering. Spring is the best time of year to divide these plants. Some gardeners contend that the plants never need dividing; whether you divide your plants or not will depend on their overall growth and how you intend to use them in your garden. To divide, cut with a sharp knife, leaving at least one eye per piece. The tuberous

Orange Kniphofia uvaria

Yellow Kniphofia uvaria

Liatris scariosa *'White Spires'*

Liriope muscari
'Big Blue'

Lobelia cardinalis

Lobelia siphilitica

roots should be planted 4 to 6 inches deep. Sow seed outdoors in early spring or summer for flowers the following summer; prechill seed in the refrigerator for several weeks. Germination takes 15 days or longer.

Uses: Borders, wildflower meadow, by watersides, cutting.

Lily turf; see *Liriope*

Liriope muscari (lee-REE-o-pay mus-KAH-ree) **lilyturf** Easy ○ ◑ ● ◗ ◖

Zones: 6 to 10
Height: 1 to 1½ feet
Colors: White, violet, mauve, lavender
Characteristics: Liriopes look like large grape hyacinths that flower at the end of summer. The plain or striped foliage of graceful, curving, grasslike leaves with leathery texture is just as decorative as the flowers. *L. muscari* is evergreen in the South, but the ravages of a northern winter require shearing damaged foliage in spring or fall. The blue-black berries that follow the flowers can be picked for late-fall arrangements. This plant will do well under a wide range of light conditions and is a good groundcover for under trees, or a decorative edging for a walk. 'Big Blue' has deep green foliage and reaches 15 inches. 'Variegata' grows 18 inches tall and has green leaves variegated in yellow.
Cultural Information: If you can provide for good drainage, *L. muscari* and its cultivars will grow in almost any soil. A neutral to slightly acid soil is preferable. They require ample moisture but can withstand short periods of drought. In cold areas,

leaves may brown in late winter, and should be cut back in spring and added to the compost pile. Divide tufted or rhizomatous plants in early spring before new growth begins. They can, however, remain undisturbed indefinitely. Self-sown seedlings may be inferior.
Uses: Cutting, border, groundcover, edging paths.

Lobelia (lo-BEL-ee-a) **cardinal flower, blue cardinal flower** Native American Moderate ○ ◑ ◖

Zones: 2 to 8
Height: 2 to 4 feet
Colors: Red, blue
Characteristics: Lobelia cardinales is as bright and handsome as a cardinal. The stately plants are covered with spikes of brilliant carmine flowers that bloom mid- to late summer. It prefers growing next to a pond or stream, where it can presumably gaze at its own reflection while keeping its feet wet. The individual flowers are small but many, growing in a spike along the upper 6 to 8 inches of the stem. They are attractive to hummingbirds. The leaves are dark green and oblong, formed opposite one another in whorls along the stalk. The stalk grows 3 to 4 feet and is topped with the brilliant flowers. The plant can be short-lived, but will self-sow where happy. *L. siphilitica* has blue flowers on bushy plants and is not as fussy as its brighter relative, growing quite happily in drier, shady spots.
Cultural Information: Plant in well-drained, sandy loam that is high in organic matter and kept evenly moist. Keep well-watered and remove faded flower

stalks to help the plants produce more (although smaller) spikes. Mulch in summer to retain moisture, and again in winter to protect the crowns. Divide by lifting the clump and removing the outside clusters of new basal growth in early fall; reset the outside clusters. If divided yearly, they will live longer. They can be grown from seeds sown in the fall, blooming the following summer.
Uses: Moist shady spots in natural gardens, good woodland or stream-side plant, long-lasting cut flowers.

Loosestrife; see *Lysimachia*

Lunaria (loon-AH-ree-a) **honesty plant, silver-dollar plant** Easy ○ ◑ ◖ ✽

Zones: 4 to 8
Height: 3 to 4 feet
Colors: Purple
Characteristics: Some grow the biennial lunaria for its spring-blooming, deep lavender-blue flowers, although it is better known for the dried seed pods that look like silver dollars. The flowers appear in April, staying through June, and are followed by silvery disc seed pods that stay on the plants all summer and make interesting winter bouquets.
Cultural Information: Lunarias are not fussy and thrive in

ordinary soil. They are easily grown from seed, planted in June for flowers the following summer. Although they are biennial, they self-sow prolifically and may become a nuisance. When cutting for drying, cut as soon as the green fades from the seed heads, and bring them inside to protect them from rain and wind.

Uses: Dried flowers, border.

Lungwort; see *Pulmonaria*

Lupine; see *Lupinus*

Lupinus (loo-PY-nus) **lupine**
Native American Easy

○ ◖ ✳ 🌡 ❀

Zones: 4 to 7
Height: 2 to 3 feet
Colors: Many solid colors and bicolors
Characteristics: In early summer, lupines send up spikes 3 (or more) feet tall, lined with pea like flowers of enchanting colors. The handsome foliage resembles the fingers of a hand. 'Russell' hybrid is the best-known variety, available in white, yellow, pink, red, salmon, lavender, blue, and purple, as well as many bicolors.
Cultural Information: Lupines grow best in cooler areas, in acid soil. Failure to thrive can often be traced to over-zealous liming. Set new plants 15 inches apart and mulch to keep the soil moist and cool. Plants start to look their best in their second year of bloom. Remove spent flowers to prevent seed formation that saps the strength of the plants. Cutting back spent flower spikes sometimes encourages more bloom in the fall. Lupines are easily increased by

dividing in early spring. Before direct sowing, nick the seed coats or soak seeds for twenty-four hours prior to sowing. Sow outdoors in spring or late summer, or indoors eight to ten weeks before setting out in early spring. Indoors, seeds will germinate in four to five weeks with 80-degree Fahrenheit day/ 75-degree Fahrenheit evening temperatures. Outdoor germination takes a little longer. Move the plants carefully outside and slowly acclimate them to outdoor temperatures, as they resent transplanting. Sowing seeds in peat pots is the best method.
Uses: Border, cutting.

Lychnis (LIK-nis) **champion**
Moderate ○ 🌡

Zones: 4 to 8
Height: 1½ to 3 feet
Colors: Scarlet, red-purple, rose-pink
Characteristics: Members of the genus *Lychnis* are some of the most brilliant of the old-fashioned flowers. These plants have been enjoyed in gardens for over three hundred years and are considered among the best plants for withstanding drought. These popular garden perennials are grown for their dense clusters of brilliantly colored flowers (the bold reds sometimes called "scarlet lightning"), now available in many softer colors. The various species have widely divergent flower forms, ranging from upright spikes to rounded heads and loose clusters. They bloom mid- to late summer and provide an elegant accompaniment to old roses and aromatic plants.
  L. chalcedonica, known as the Maltese Cross, has bright red

flowers. *L. coronaria* is the favored rose companion, planted in front of old roses where its woolly, silvery leaves contrast with the green foliage of the roses. 'Oculta' is a bicolor with white blooms with conspicuous, cherry red eyes.
  L. viscaria, German catch fly, features rose-red, 18-inch flowers in June. It gets its common name from the sticky sap under the flower head that traps insects.
Cultural Information: Plant *Lychnis* species in moist or dampish, well-drained soil in spring or fall 10 to 15 inches apart. Remove spent flowers to encourage longer bloom season and secondary bloom in August. Divide plants every third or fourth year, in spring or fall when the clumps become crowded, if smaller clumps or more plants are wanted. As a rule, clumps may remain undisturbed indefinitely. Sow seeds outdoors in spring, summer, or fall. They will flower the first year if started early indoors, germinating in three to four weeks at 70 degrees Fahrenheit. Do not cover seeds, as they need light to germinate. Seedlings are difficult to transplant as they don't like their roots disturbed. It is best to start them in peat pots.
Uses: Border, cutting.

Lysimachia (li-si-MAK-ee-a) **loosestrife** Easy
○ ◑ 🌡 ❀

Zones: 4 to 9
Height: 2½ to 3 feet
Colors: White, yellow
Characteristics: Many members of the genus *Lysimachia* are showy garden plants, easy to grow, old-fashioned, and excel-

Lunaria

Lupinus polyphyllus
'Russell Hybrid Mixed'

Lychnis

Lysimachia clethroides

Lysimachia punctata

Lysimachia nummularia

lent where they can run wild without overrunning less vigorous plants. These plants bloom in early to late summer, depending on the variety.

L. clethroides has graceful, curving white spikes, resembling a gooseneck or shepherd's crook, and blooms in midsummer. (I once planted it at the end of the perennial garden, where it held the evening light beautifully. Later I discovered it traveled underground at the speed of light, marching over and destroying neighboring plants. I moved it to a wilder area where it can run, but every year in my perennial border I continue to dig up long taproots that jump up in new places.) Any piece of root left in the ground is capable of forming a new plant.

L. nummularia, or Creeping Jenny, is shallow-rooted and spreading—but not a troublemaker. It is delightful growing along a stream where it can dangle in the water, or draped over rocks. It blooms with bright yellow, fragrant, small flowers in early summer. The cultivar 'Aurea' has yellowish leaves but insignificant flowers.

L. punctata is a tall, spiky plant covered with yellow flowers in midsummer. It likes moist, shady places and has naturalized along country roads, earning it the name of "ditch witch."
Cultural Information: All garden varieties are best if planted in moist, rich soil, but average soil is satisfactory if it retains moisture. Otherwise, add peat moss or compost, and water during dry spells. Taller varieties may need supports. Plants can be divided in the spring. Sow seeds in early spring.
Uses: Border, cutting, wildflower garden, woodland walk.

Lythrum salicaria

(LITH-rum sal-i-SAH-ree-a) **purple loosestrife** Easy

◑ ○ ◆ ✹ ❚ ❀

Zones: 3 to 9
Height: 1½ to 6 feet
Colors: Purple, pink, magenta
Characteristics: Purple loosestrife is a plant that caused much trouble in its early escape from the garden to naturalize along highways in the northern United States. Although it is a beautiful sight to drive by fields of purple loosestrife, this plant is crowding out and destroying native wildflowers. Today's hybrids, related to roadside loosestrife, are nevertheless better behaved, more compact, and easily contained in the garden because they are sterile and don't produce seed. 'Morden's Pink' is a popular variety, with rose-pink flowers on plants 3 to 4 feet tall. These long spires of closely set, small, deep pink flowers bloom from erect stems, midsummer to early fall, all

the while withstanding neglect. They are trouble-free and long-lived.
Cultural Information: Purple loosestrife grows in ordinary soil but is tolerant of wet areas and suitable for wild settings. The plants grow large and bushy, so space 24 inches apart. Divide in spring or fall, using a sharp knife or even an axe, as the roots can be difficult to separate. The cultivars should be started by nursery plants or divisions. Seed-grown plants will vary considerably.
Uses: Border, cutting, drying.

Mallow; see *Malva*

Malva sylvestris (MAL-va

sil-VES-tris) **mallow, Billy buttons** Moderate ○ ❚ ❀
Zones: 3 to 9
Height: 2 to 4 feet
Colors: White, pink
Characteristics: The buds of *M. sylvestris* look like so many tightly rolled, pink party favors —before they open to full, five-petaled, hollyhocklike flowers. A wildflower in Europe, it is not as widely grown here as its accommodating manners and unstinting, long bloom deserve. A good plant for short, northern summers, it continues to bloom after heavy frost. It is fast-growing, short-lived, and self-sowing. The flowers open in summer or early fall. 'Zebra', a favorite, has light pink flowers with darker, rose-veined markings radiating from the center.
Cultural Information: Well-drained soil is best, but the plant will tolerate heavy, clay soils. It readily reseeds and doesn't need staking. It thrives in hot climates only if the soil

is deep, moist, humus-enriched, and free of tree roots. Light afternoon shade is recommended where summers are hot. The seeds are shaped like little loaves of bread or cheeses, which explains some of the old-fashioned common names. Check in the spring for self-sown seedlings grown up at the base of the plants. These seedlings are easily transplanted and the best way to increase your plants. Seeds can be started early indoors to be planted into the garden (12 inches apart) after danger of frost.
Uses: Border, cutting.

Meadow sage; see *Salvia*

Michealmas daisy; see *Aster*

Milkweed; see *Asclepias*

Mist flower; see *Eupatorium*

Monarda (mo-NAR-da) **bee balm, bergamot, Oswego tea** Native American Easy ◑ ○ 🌡 ❀
Zones: 4 to 9
Height: 2 to 3 feet
Colors: Pink, purple, white, red
Characteristics: Monardas invite hummingbirds to a feast of nectar every midsummer day. The bushy clusters of erect stems are topped with fluffy, dense heads of small, tubular flowers arranged in whorls. The leaves are lush (aromatic when crushed) and attractive all season. Monardas spread rapidly, blooming from late June into August. They are handsome members of the mint family and, when steeped in boiling water, their fragrant leaves produce a re-

freshing drink—hence the name Oswego tea. Blooming time can be stretched to eight weeks or more if the flowers are removed before they go to seed. Some of the best cultivars for the garden are 'Snow White' for creamy white flowers, 'Blue Stocking' for violet-blue, 'Cambridge Scarlet' for scarlet and 'Croftway Pink' for soft pink.
Cultural Information: As monardas spread, their stems become sparse, tall, and lanky. The remedy is to divide every three years. This will also ensure maximum bloom. Dividing is best done in the spring. The plants prefer moist soil rich in organic matter and of average fertility. Deprived of moisture, they become more susceptible to such diseases as powdery mildew. In shady areas and rich soil, they become vigorous and spread rampantly by means of underground stems. Careful placement is important to prevent crowding out other plants. Space plants 12 to 15 inches apart. Sow seeds outdoors in spring or fall for bloom the following season. Germination takes one to two weeks.
Uses: Cutting, border, wild garden, woodland walk.

Monkshood; see *Aconitum*

Moss pinks; see *Phlox subulata*

Mountain blue; see *Centaurea*

Mountain pinks; see *Phlox subulata*

Mugwort; see *Artemesia*

Mums; see *Chrysanthemum*

Nepeta (NE-pe-ta) **catmint, catnip** Easy ○ ◑ 🌟 🌡 ❀
Zones: 3 to 9
Height: 1½ to 2 feet
Colors: Lavender-blue
Characteristics: Nepeta are somewhat sprawling plants with small, gray-green leaves and 5-inch spikes of lavender flowers that bloom in early summer and often into fall. Cats love the smell of the foliage of *N. cataria* and will often roll, play, and sleep on them, but the plants are tough and, though they may become matted, recover easily. *N.* × *faassenii* is an 18-inch-high, tough plant that makes an attractive groundcover, blooming for several months in the summer.
Cultural Information: Plants should be spaced 1½ feet apart to allow them room to spread. They prefer sandy soil, but will grow in almost any soil enriched with compost and having good drainage. Shear plants back after first bloom to encourage further flowering. They seldom need support. Divide in spring or take cuttings in summer to

Lythrum salicaria 'Morden's Pink'

Malva moschata

Nepeta faassenii

Monarda didyma 'Croftway Pink'

Oenothera speciosa

Paeonia 'Red Charm'

Paeonia 'Pink Parfait'

Paeonia 'Cora Stubbs'

increase your plants. Cat lovers can sow seeds of *N. cataria*, but the ornamental *N. faassenii* sets no seeds.

Uses: Seaside garden, front of a border, edger, groundcover, rock garden.

Obedient plant; see **Physostegia**

Oenothera (ee-no-THEE-ra) **evening primrose** Native American Easy ○ ◗ ☀
Zones: 4 to 8
Height: 10 inches to 2 feet
Colors: Satiny pink, yellow, white
Characteristics: Oenotheras are called evening primroses be-

cause they customarily open in the late afternoon or evening, and fade by morning. Once the floral display is over, the foliage continues to look attractive and takes on an autumn rosy tint. The showy, single flowers are 1½ inches across and appear in early to midsummer over a period of several weeks.

Oenothera missouriensis is commonly called Ozark sundrops because its yellow, cup-shaped flowers, up to 5 inches across, are wildflowers in the Ozark Mountains. These are tough, spreading plants. *O. speciosa*, the showy, pink evening primrose, has naturalized along Texas roadsides and in meadows where it creates fields of what looks like cotton candy. This species tends to spread in the home garden but is easy to control. In my garden, several plants drape over a stone wall and bloom all summer.

Cultural Information: These carefree plants are drought-resistant and tolerant of poor soil, spreading rampantly in good soil. They tolerate high humidity and heat. They can be propagated by seed, cuttings, or division in early spring. Plant out in the garden 12 to 15 inches apart in a well-drained, light soil.
Uses: Front of border, rock garden, meadow.

Oswego tea; see *Monarda*

Paeonia (pie-ON-ee-a) **peony** Easy ○ ◐ ☀ ⬥
Zones: 3 to 8
Height: 2 to 4 feet
Colors: White, pink, crimson, red, coral, bicolors

Characteristics: Brought to Europe in the 1700s from China and Siberia, where they had been cultivated for centuries, peonies are the cornerstone of the late spring garden. They may feature single, semidouble, or double flowers, and come in many sumptuous shades. Don't overlook the beauty of the single, nor its ability to close and survive heavy rains, to hold its head up higher and to provide more blooms then the heavier doubles. From the first crimson shoots that emerge in early spring to the last bronze-tinged leaves in autumn, the foliage remains handsome. Once established in well-drained soil and the proper setting, peonies put on a show for many years, producing fragrant flowers as valuable for cutting as for garden display. Plants take very little care, mature about three to five years from planting, and last a lifetime. Some gardeners contend they should be planted alone for the best garden effect, giving them lots of sunshine and good air circulation, since they prefer not to be crowded. Others insist they share space, as a companion plant in the perennial border. (I have a lilac and peony walk leading to the vegetable garden. The lilacs bloom with the peonies, complementing them in both color and form. Each clump of peonies is a different color, starting with white, moving through pinks into coral, then deep pink, scarlet, and returning to white.) Their bloom times vary from early, to mid, to late season. If properly planned, succession bloom can continue for four to six weeks.

Cultural Information: Plant peonies in full sun in rich, well-drained soil about 2 to 3 feet apart. Pick an area protected from strong wind. Cover the eyes with soil 1½ inches deep and mulch their first winter for protection. Cut the foliage back to soil level in the fall. Division isn't necessary but you can divide after three or four years in late summer or early fall to increase your clump, making sure to leave three to five eyes per division. Water your plants regularly especially during dry spells. The plants like to be fed in the spring with a low nitrogen slow release fertilizer, 8–8–8, but do not let fresh manure or fast-acting nitrogen come in direct contact with their fleshy roots. Too much nitrogen will reduce the number of flowers and increase the amount of foliage. Peonies don't perform well in the subtropic regions of the Southwest and Southeast, as they require some winter cold for dormancy. If growing in Zone 8 it is best to select earlier-blooming types with single flowers. The earlier the bloom and the cooler the weather, the longer the flower lasts. Varieties with single flowers are susceptible to fewer diseases caused by heat, humidity, and rain trapped between their petals. Start from nursery plants or divisions planted in late August or early September.
Uses: Borders, cutting, landscape accent.

Painted daisy; see *Chrysanthemum*

Papaver orientale

(pa-PAY-ver o-ree-en-TAH-lee) **Oriental poppy** Moderate

○ ◑ ✳ ⬙

Zones: 3 to 7
Height: 16 inches to 4 feet
Colors: Scarlet, orange, white, rose, crimson, salmon
Characteristics: "Here today, gone tomorrow" characterizes the quick-growing, blooming, and disappearing act of the Oriental poppy. This delightful perennial has a rightful place in the garden even though the May–June flowering period is of short duration. Its vibrant orange-red flowers are easily spotted, even at a distance, so plan where you plant. Oriental poppies should be combined with such perennials as *Gypsophila* or *Perovskia*, which spread their flowers in July to cover the dying foliage and, later, the empty space left by poppies. Each flower has purplish-black blotches at its base and a tufted black center, which sets off the bright flower colors. Oriental poppies make a striking display when in bloom, their flowers having a translucent, crinkled paper texture, usually with four to six petals. The foliage is coarse and hairy, borne on bushy plants; individual leaves are feather-shaped, with a leaflet on either side. 'Allegro' has scarlet red flowers on 16-inch plants. 'Brilliant Red' is a dazzling, taller poppy, 28 to 30 inches and makes a focal point in the garden or perennial border.
Cultural Information: Culture of this plant is somewhat challenging at first, since it does not appreciate being transplanted. It takes a season or two to mature but, once established, it is spectacular in the garden. Like most perennials, Oriental poppies have a dormant period; for Oriental poppies it is around mid-July to October. New foliage will appear in the fall and persist through winter. Set roots 3 to 4 inches deep and 18 to 24 inches apart in rich, well-drained soil. Clumps of foliage expand and sometimes reach 3 feet wide. This plant performs best in regions of cool summers and is short-lived in warm-winter areas. Mulch it in summer to cool the soil and moisten roots. Be careful not to damage roots with cultivation in late summer after foliage has died down. Taller plants may require staking. Divide during the dormant period by taking a 6-inch root cutting. Put cuttings back in the soil to a depth of 1 inch and new leaves should appear in about one month. It will take plants propagated in this fashion about two years to bloom.
Uses: Cutting, border, accent.

Peony; see *Paeonia*

Perennial cornflower; see *Centaurea*

Papaver orientale
'Allegro'

Papaver orientale *'Show Girl'*

Above: Perovskia atriplicifolia. *Below:* Phlox divaricata.

Below: Phlox paniculata *'Starfire'*

Perovskia atriplicifolia
(pe-ROF-skee-a   a-tri-plis-i-FO-lee-a)
Russian sage Easy
○ ◔ ✳ ▮ ✿
Zones: 5 to 9
Height: 2½ to 3 feet
Colors: Lavender-blue
Characteristics: Equally valuable for its handsome silvery foliage and for the fragrant, small, tubular blue flowers that appear in mid- to late summer, Russian sage is a fine shrubbery perennial, excellent toward the back of the border or planted singly as an accent. The lavender-blue flowers are offset by stems covered with a white down and gray-green foliage. The flowers are long-lasting for cutting. Combine Russian sage with fall-blooming pink asters, white boltonias or yellow chrysanthemums for a late summer garden.
Cultural Information: This plant grows best in well-drained, average soil. The shrublike stems may die back to the ground in the North, but come back from the roots. A good plant to withstand drought in areas of low rainfall. Propagation can be done by taking stem cuttings in summer.
Uses: Cutting, back of border, accent.

Phlox divaricata (flox di-vah-ri-KAH-ta) **woodland phlox**
Native American Easy
◑ ✳ ▮ ✿
Zones: 3 to 8
Height: 8 to 12 inches
Characteristics: 'Fuller's White' is a lovely form of the North American native wild phlox. Among the finest of plants to naturalize on open woodland, it establishes colonies 8 to 12 inches high with loosely clustered white flowers from April to June. The flowers completely cover the plant. This is a very desirable and garden-worthy plant for the partly shaded border, a good companion for spring-blooming bulbs.
Cultural Information: Plant individual plants about 12 inches apart. They prefer moist, but well-drained, soil enriched with compost or leaf mulch. Plants can be divided in late summer.
Uses: Shady border, woodland walk.

Phlox paniculata (flox pa-nik-ew-LAH-ta) **garden phlox**
Native American Easy
○ ◑ ▮ ✿
Zones: 3 to 9
Height: 30 to 36 inches
Colors: White, pink, red, violet-blue
Characteristics: The mainstay of the late-summer perennial garden is *P. paniculata*, with the brightest, most varied range of colors. It is the best-known phlox of all, bearing huge clusters of sweetly scented flowers from early summer through fall. Easy to grow, it produces a strong, bushy habit and reaches full maturity about two years after planting. This phlox is best suited to the back of the perennial border and makes an excellent companion for monkshood and *Cimicifuga*. Its large flower heads and long stems make hardy garden phlox an exceptionally valuable cut flower. It is better in northern gardens since it is not very heat-tolerant. 'Dodo Hanbury Forbes' is a bicolor of pink florets with red eyes. 'Princess' is all white, 'Progress' has soft lavender florets with blue-purple eyes and 'Starfire' is a rich red.
Cultural Information: Set plants 15 to 18 inches apart in full sun, in a rich, well-drained but moisture-retentive soil enriched with organic matter. Planting should be done in spring. Faded blooms must be removed to prevent seed formation and to encourage more bloom. When plants are well established, pinch back the weaker shoots to ground level for stronger stems, or thin each clump to four or five shoots and space the new shoots 4 to 6 inches apart to get the largest possible flower clusters. Plants will run out (go out of bloom) if not divided. Divide in fall or spring when plants are four to five years old. They need proper spacing for good air flow, and are very susceptible to powdery mildew in areas of high humidity. If one cultivar doesn't do well in your garden, try another. Mulch in winter with 3-inch layer of hay, straw, or pine branches.
Uses: Cutting, back of border.

Phlox stolonifera (flox sto-lo-NI-fe-ra) **creeping phlox** Native American Easy

◖ ✳ ✿

Zones: 4 to 8
Height: 6 to 12 inches
Colors: Pink, blue, white
Characteristics: A low-growing, native North American plant, with attractive, paddle-shaped leaves and 1-inch, five-petaled flowers in late spring. Excellent for groundcover, in the front of the border or, better yet, naturalized in open woodland.
Cultural Information: Creeping phlox thrives in soil of high organic content, where it rapidly establishes luxuriant colonies. Plant 1 foot apart in the fall to allow the roots more time to become established before flowering. This variety is more shade-tolerant than most other phloxes.
Uses: Woodland walk, shady border.

Phlox subulata (flox soob-ew-LAH-ta) **mountain pinks, moss pinks, ground pinks, ground phlox** Native American Easy

○ ◖ ✳ ✿

Zones: 2 to 9
Height: 4 to 6 inches
Colors: Blue, pink, red, white
Characteristics: This early-flowering beauty welcomes spring with plants literally covered with blossoms, hiding their needle-like leaves. *Phlox subulata* is a rock-garden favorite, especially the fluorescent pink varieties, which make attractive edgers and groundcovers. They give the most effective display when massed in groups of three or more. You can expect a few blooms the first season, but this lovely, long-blooming plant generally takes two to three years to reach peak size. The foliage is evergreen in warmer areas. *P. subulata* spreads rapidly. It blooms in April and May. There are many varieties, available in many colors. 'Atropurpurea' is rosy red, 'Blue Emerald' is lavender-blue, and 'Coral Eye' is pink with a red eye.
Cultural Information: Space plants 8 to 12 inches apart in average to moderately dry, well-drained soil (soil should be more acid than pH 6.0). After flowers fade, plants should be sheared back about halfway. This will keep the plants from spreading and most likely plants will develop new foliage and a few blooms in the fall. Divide in spring after flowering every two to three years, or when plants look overcrowded or are not blooming as profusely.
Uses: Rock gardens, edgers, groundcovers.

Physalis alkekengii

(FISS-a-lis al-ke-KEN-jee-ee) **Chinese lantern** Easy ○ ◖ 🌡 ✿
Zones: 3 to 10
Height: 2 feet
Colors: Orange
Characteristics: An interesting plant grown for its seemingly inflated, orange-red, lantern-shaped seed coverings. The pods are papery and shaped like Chinese lanterns, hence the common name.

The plant's inconspicuous white flowers come into bloom in the summer. After pollination they produce hollow, green seed pods that turn orange-red towards fall. Dark green leaves usually hide the tiny white blooms. Plants will grow 2 feet tall with a branching habit. For use in winter bouquets, cut the stems in the fall when the "lanterns" are just starting to turn color. Remove leaves, tie several stems together, and hang them upside-down in a well-ventilated, dark place. It will take several weeks for them to dry properly. Stems hung upside-down will dry straight.
Cultural Information: Average, well-drained soil is important, but fertilizer isn't needed; in fact, the plant may grow too rapidly if fed or grown in rich soils. Set the crown level with the soil line in a hole large enough to accommodate the roots without crowding. Firm the soil gently around the roots. Water the plant well to eliminate any air pockets that may form around the roots. Set plants 1½ to 2 feet apart in rows spaced 3 to 3½ feet apart. Because *P. alkekengii* is a rampant grower, you may wish to confine it in a separate garden area. New transplants should be well-watered. Additional water is a good idea during periods of dry weather. Plants may remain undisturbed indefinitely. If clumps become overcrowded, root cuttings or clump divisions may be made in the fall or spring. All will produce "lanterns" during the first growing season. Chinese lanterns may be grown from seed as an annual, flowering and fruiting in one season.
Uses: Border, woodland walk, cutting, drying.

Physostegia (fy-so-STEE-jee-a) **obedient plant, false dragonhead** Native American Easy

○ ◖ 🌡 ✿

Phlox subulata

Above: Phlox stolonifera *'Homefires'*
Below: Physalis alkekengii.

Zones: 3 to 9
Height: 2 to 3 feet
Colors: White, pink
Characteristics: Members of the genus *Physostegia* are called "obedient plant" because their individual flowers stay put when gently pushed to either side of the stem. The plants themselves lack manners and spread, crowding out other plants. They are handsome, clump-forming perennials, excellent for cutting and showy in the border at summer's end. From midsummer to early fall, spikes of small, tubular flowers appear in profusion. The leaves are small and neat.
Cultural Information: Physostegias are easy to grow in a sunny location in a moisture-retentive soil. Plant 15 to 18 inches apart, as the plants spread rapidly. Divide every three years in spring, saving only outer portions of each clump. Physostegias prefer an acid pH but otherwise are not really particular about soil. Water regularly during dry spells. Sow seeds in spring.
Uses: Cutting, borders.

Pincushion flower; see *Scabiosa*

Pinks; see *Dianthus*

Plantain lily; see *Hosta*

Platycodon (plat-i-KO-don)
balloon flower Easy
○ ◑ ❘ ✿ ❋
Zones: 3 to 9
Height: 2 to 3 feet
Colors: White, rich blue, pink
Characteristics: Balloon flowers are long-lived, slow-growing, and well-behaved plants for the sunny border. Their puffy buds look first like little balloons, then open into star-shaped flowers that make lavish displays from June to frost. The leaves are oval-shaped, 1 to 2 inches long and of medium green with a bluish underside. The flowers are available in single and double varieties, and all make long-lasting cut flowers.
Cultural Information: Since balloon flowers are late to break dormancy in the spring, be careful not to dig them up accidentally before they put in an appearance. The plants are long-lived, provided the soil drains well. Their fleshy roots make division difficult, and they resent disturbance. Division can be done for propagation in the spring, but be careful as transplanting isn't always successful. Cut away the outer portion of the crown, retaining as many roots and buds as possible. Plant the divisions thickly to safeguard against failures. Set crowns so they are barely covered with soil. Removing faded flowers will extend the bloom season. Staking may be required for tall plants. Balloon flowers can be started from seeds but will not flower for two to three years. Sow seeds in spring or late summer; do not cover with soil.
Uses: Borders, arrangements, cutting.

Primrose; see *Primula*

Primula (PRIM-yew-la) **primrose** Easy ◑ ○ ✳ ❘ ❋
Zones: 4 to 7
Height: 6 inches to 2 feet
Colors: Many colors
Characteristics: Primulas are among the most charming of all spring-blooming perennials. Plant them in groups in the woodland garden mixed with spring bulbs, at the edges of shaded beds, or under the shade of evergreens in informal foundation plantings.
Primula denticulata 'Alba' has rounded heads of dainty, pure white flowers atop 10- to 12-inch stems. *P. polyantha* 'Dwarf Jewel' has compact clumps of bright green leaves surrounded by clusters of brightly colored flowers. *P. japonica* plants are aptly named "candelabra primroses," as they rise up from 12 to 24 inches and flower in turns at the top of the stem. If you have been given a potted primrose, enjoy it first as a houseplant and later, when the weather warms, plant it in the garden for next year's bloom.

Plant tufts of primroses with yellow marsh marigolds and sheets of forget-me-nots. All will delight in spreading along the banks of a brook or throughout low, wet land. (Blue flag irises love to have their feet wet and can be used as punctuation marks in the planting.)
Cultural Information: Plant primroses in moisture-retentive soil that has been enriched with organic matter. A winter mulch is beneficial in colder climates. Divide as they get crowded, every two to three years, in late spring or summer immediately after flowering. Sow seeds in spring or fall. They grow best where spring temperatures are cool.
Uses: Woodland garden, edges of shaded beds, along ponds, streams, or bogs.

Pulmonaria (pul-mon-AH-ree-a)
lungwort Easy

● ◑ ✳ 🌡 ❀

Zones: 3 to 8
Height: 12 inches
Colors: Blue, pink, pink turning to blue, white spotted leaves, white
Characteristics: In my Zone 7 garden, I have had flowers nodding from small pulmonarias in mid-February. Unlike other plants which grow foliage first and flower only after the plant is close to its mature size, pulmonarias flower early, when the leaves are only an inch long. Through the season, as the leaves grow, the flowers bloom. By the time the flowers stop blooming, the plants have increased their size by several times; the leaves continue to grow to 5 or more inches by summer's end.

Pulmonaria angustifolia, 'Azurea' has deep green leaves with clusters of pink buds that open, then change to a rich, pure blue. *P. saccharata*, 'Mrs. Moon' is my favorite because of its silvery spots on the dark green leaves. Even without flowers, it lights up a shady spot. These early-blooming plants are particularly valuable in shade and partial shade as groundcovers and for naturalizing. They have dainty, drooping clusters of small, blue flowers, blooming from early through late spring, and the leaves are attractive all season. 'Sissinghurst White' has white-splotched foliage and white flowers.
Cultural Information: Plant pulmonarias in moist, cool soil high in organic content. Plant 1 foot apart, as the plants spread rapidly. Divide the plants in late summer or early spring. Division is not required, but is an excellent means of increasing clumps. Water well after dividing the plants and continue to water all fall until the ground freezes.
Uses: Groundcover, borders, naturalizing, woodland walk.

Rainbow rock cress; see *Aubrieta*

Red-hot poker; see *Kniphofia*

Red valerian; see *Centranthus*

Rudbeckia (rood-BEK-ee-a)
black-eyed Susan Native American Easy

○ ◗ ✺ 🌡 ❀

Zones: 3 to 9
Height: 2 to 4 feet
Colors: Golden yellow, orange, red, bronze
Characteristics: The most showy, daisylike flowers of summer, rudbeckias provide garden color all summer and lots of long-lasting cut flowers. *Rudbeckia hirta* 'Gloriosa Daisy' has profuse displays of huge blooms, up to 5 inches across, on long (3-foot) stems. The range of colors includes yellow, orange, red, bronze, and attractive combinations of these all surrounding and set off by a central dark prominant cone. *R. fulgida* 'Goldsturm' has 2-foot plants laden with 3- to 4-inch deep yellow flowers surrounding rich dark centers. *R. fulgida* 'Speciosa' is a long-blooming variety—June to October—with golden flowers and chocolate centers.
Cultural Information: Plant rudbeckias 2 feet apart in well-drained, moist soil of average fertility. Divide them in spring every four to five years to keep the plants blooming freely. Planting from nursery stock or divisions in spring is best, although you can sow seeds in spring to bloom the following year. These plants are tolerant of poor soil, winter's cold, and summer's extreme heat.
Uses: Cutting, border, meadow.

Purple loosestrife; see *Lythrum*

Russian sage; see *Perovskia*

Salvia (SAL-vee-a) **meadow sage** Native American Easy

○ ◗ ✺ 🌡 ❀

Zones: 4 to 9
Height: 1½ to 4 feet
Colors: Blues—violet, lavender, sky blue
Characteristics: These salvias are covered with spikes of intense violet-blue blooms for long periods in the summer. Their leaves stay attractive all season long and are aromatic when crushed. Their fragrance repels rabbits.

Salvia azurea, with pale, sky-blue flowers is native from South Carolina to Florida and Texas. *S. pitcheri*, a darker blue, is common in the central states. Both bloom in September, to reach 3 to 4 feet in height; they are at their finest when grown in masses and planted close together. *S. superba* 'East Friesland' is 18 inches tall and

Above: Pulmonaria saccharata 'Mrs. Moon'.
Below: Rudbeckia fulgida 'Goldsturm Strain'.

Opposite, from top: Physostegia virginiana 'Vivid'; Platycodon grandiflorus 'Mariesii'; Primula x polyantha 'Dwarf Jewel'; Primula japonica.

Salvia superba 'Verbena'

Saponaria officinalis
'Rubra Plena'

Scabiosa caucasica
'Fama'

covered with spikes of intense violet-blue blooms from early June into September. Plant it with yellow coreopsis for a long, summer display.

One of the most beautiful of the blue salvias is *S. pratensis*, a native of Greece; it produces whorled spikes of blue-violet flowers with abandon all summer. Its only drawback is its short lifespan.
Cultural Information: Plant salvias 18 inches apart in any soil that is well-drained and of average fertility, and it will be long-lived. It stays in place, forming clumps. It will withstand heat, drought, and poor soil well. However, wet soil during the winter is very often fatal. Salvias are especially good for southern states but will be successful in northern areas with winter snow or mulch protection from the freezing and thawing of winter weather.
Uses: Cutting, dried flowers, border.

Saponaria officinalis

(sa-po-NAH-ree-a o-fi-si-NAH-lis)
double bouncing bet Easy
○ ❚
Zones: 3 to 9
Height: 2½ feet
Colors: Pink
Characteristics: Fragrance and beauty combine in this wonderful double-flowered form of an old-time favorite. It forms impressive colonies, with each plant about 2½ feet tall and spreading to 3 feet in diameter, covered almost all summer with double-pink, phloxlike flowers. The flowers are particularly effective when their fragrance develops at night.

Cultural Information: Plant double bouncing bet 1 foot apart in spring in well-drained soil. Water once per week until the roots are established, then more sparingly until the plants flower well. Divide clumps every three years in fall or spring. The plants may need staking, as the weight of the flowers sometimes causes them to tumble over.
Uses: Rockeries, border, cutting.

Scabiosa caucasica

(skab-i-O-sa kaw-CA-si-ka) **pincushion flower** Moderately Easy
○ ✳ ❚ ❀
Zones: 2 to 9
Height: 2½ feet
Colors: Blue, white
Characteristics: The pincushion is so named because its globular heads of flowers have protruding stigmas that resemble pins in a pin cushion. It flowers from early summer into fall. The foliage is large and dense at the base of the plant but becomes sparse and smaller on the stem. The stems grow in clusters and appear open and loose. This is a long-lived plant with long-blooming flowers and restrained growth. Some of the better varieties are 'Blue Snowflake' for blue flowers and 'Miss Willmott' for white.
Cultural Information: Space plants 10 to 15 inches apart in a sunny location where the soil is preferably alkaline, light loam, and moist in summer but well-drained in winter. Plants rot and die in heavy soils and bloom only sporadically in hot, humid weather. In southern climates a location in light shade can prove helpful. Remove faded flowers to prolong bloom. Plants may

require staking, depending on their location. Divide clumps to maintain vigor in spring when they start to deteriorate; division is an excellent means of increasing the number of plants. Seeds can be sown early spring through summer for bloom the following year. Germination takes one to two weeks. They may bloom at the end of the first season if sown early enough indoors and then transplanted out after all danger of frost. Sow freshly collected seeds outdoors in early fall.
Uses: Borders, cutting.

Sedum

(SEE-dum) **stonecrop** Easy
○ ◑ ◊ ✸ ❀
Zones: 3 to 9
Height: 3 inches to 2 feet
Colors: Yellow, red, pink, white
Characteristics: These easy-to-grow, succulent plants thrive in sun in even the worst of soils. The genus name comes from *sedo*, meaning to sit, which aptly describes the manner in which some of the plants attach themselves to walls and crevices between rocks. Both foliage and flowers are attractive, the latter to butterflies as well. Sedums have fleshy leaves with large clusters of small flowers in summer or early fall. They are considered evergreens, blooming June through July or August through October, depending on the variety.

Sedum purpureum, 'Autumn Joy' is widely acclaimed by experts as one of the ten best perennials because it has year 'round value in the border. It quickly forms a handsome, 2-foot-tall clump of silver-green leaves, beautiful the entire summer. In midsummer, large, flat heads of light green flowers appear; gradually they change to pink, then rose, salmon-bronze, and finally coppery red as autumn advances. The dead flowers hold their shape and can look good all winter on the plants, if not beaten down by heavy snow. The flowers can be picked for dried bouquets that will last all winter.

S. cauticolum is a compact 6-inch plant with unique blue foliage and pink flowers borne all summer. It is excellent as an edging plant and in rock gardens.

S. spurium 'Dragon's Blood' is only 3 to 4 inches high, with bronze stems and star-shaped, crimson flowers from June to September. The dark green foliage turns red-bronze in autumn. Excellent as an edging plant, in the rock garden, and as a groundcover in dry areas with poor soil; many more varieties are available. Keep your eyes and ears open for new sedums to try.

Cultural Information: These plants are not fussy, growing in any well-drained soil. Wet soils, especially in winter, will cause crown rot. Sedums are very tolerant of drought. Divide your plants in spring to maintain good flowering or to increase your number of plants; note that they can go many years without requiring division for rejuvenation. Take stem cuttings any time of year as sedum roots easily. Sow seeds in late summer or midspring at 65 degrees Fahrenheit.
Uses: Massed in borders, rock gardens, between stones of a low wall, cutting, drying.

Shasta daisy; see ***Chrysanthemum***

Silver dollar plant; see ***Lunaria.***

Snowbank; see ***Boltonia***

Snow-in-summer; see ***Cerastium***

Spanish bayonet; see ***Yucca***

Speedwell; see ***Veronica***

Stachys (STA-kis) **lamb's ears** Easy ○ ◑
Zones: 4 to 9
Height: 1 to 1½ feet
Colors: Grown for silver foliage
Characteristics: Stachys byzantina is a low, tufted plant grown for its attractive leaves, furry and an intense, silvery blue-gray in color. I always feel they want to be petted. The flowers are about ½-inch long and form whorls at the top of 4- to 6-inch spikes blooming July through September. The leaves are arranged in low clumps 6 to 12 inches high, often spreading to 24 inches wide. The clumps expand slowly, but the center dies after several years and division is necessary; cut out and discard the center of the clump. *Stachys* is long-lived, neat, and restrained in growth.

Lamb's ears are good companions to offset the colors of other flowers, notably blue flowers of *Platycodon* or the pink-to-rose of *Sedum* 'Autumn Joy'. *S. byzantina* 'Silver Carpet' is one of the finest of all silver-leafed

plants for carpeting. This non-flowering form grows 18 inches high with a spread of 1 foot, forming a dense mat of woolly leaves. *S.* will tolerate partial shade and has an interesting nettlelike, showy, violet-purple flower good for cutting; it lacks the silver foliage and features green, scalloped leaves instead. *S. lanata* can be invasive, particularly in rich soil.
Cultural Information: Plant lamb's ears in well-drained soil of average fertility. *Stachys* species are prone to rotting in humid, muggy climates. Divide in spring, after the fourth year of bloom, to rejuvenate and for increase. Sow seeds outdoors in midspring or indoors in early spring at 65 degrees Fahrenheit. Germination takes less than a week.
Uses: Cutting, front of border, edger, groundcover.

St. John's wort; see ***Hypericum***

Stokes' aster; see ***Stokesia***

Stokesia (STOKE-see-a) **Stokes' aster** Native American Moderate ○ 🌡
Zones: 5 to 9
Height: 1 to 1½ feet
Colors: Blues, from deep to lilac to light, white
Characteristics: This looks like a cross between a pincushion flower and an aster, resulting in cornlike flowers 2 to 3 inches across, appearing on slender stems in mid- to late summer. They have an outer row or two of ray florets and a center of fuzzy-looking disc florets of the

Sedum 'Ruby Glow'

Sedum 'Autumn Joy'

Stachys olympica 'Silver Carpet'

Stokesia laevis

Trollius × cultorum

Verbascum

same color. Large basal clumps of lance-shaped leaves support many flower stalks. Provided with the right soil, it is long-lived. The original wild flower was native to South Carolina and further south to Louisiana and Florida. 'Blue Moon', with its large blue-lavender flowers, is one of my favorites.

Cultural Information: Space plants 12 to 15 inches apart in well-drained soil. They are intolerant of wet soil in the winter. Divide plants every three to four years—as they become crowded—in spring. Sow seeds outdoors in April or make root cuttings in summer to increase your plants.

Uses: Cutting, border.

Stonecrop; see *Sedum*

Tickseed; see *Coreopsis*

Torch lily; see *Kniphofia*

Trollius (TRO-lee-us) **globe-flower** Easy ○ ◑ ◣ ❀

Zones: 3 to 8
Height: 2 to 3 feet
Colors: Shades of yellow and orange
Characteristics: Another genus of the buttercup family (*Ranunculaceae*). Species have large single or double flowers, each composed of five to fifteen showy sepals in a rounded ball shape that always appears as though it has never fully opened. The flowers bloom on long stems in May and June. The stems grow in upright clusters, creating bushy, rounded plants. The fo-

liage remains attractive all season. The plants are long-lived in moist conditions and always restrained in growth. The clumps gradually expand by sending up new shoots on the outside edge of the crown. They are long-lasting cut flowers.

Cultural Information: Plant globe-flowers in partial shade, in moist soil that has had plenty of compost or peat moss worked in. Remove any faded flowers to prolong the bloom period. Keep the plants well-watered—never let them dry out. The plants will multiply slowly and do not need division to reduce crowding for five to six years. Divide plants late in summer or early in spring as an excellent means of increasing the numbers. Sow seeds in late summer; freeze them for two days, then plant outdoors. Fresh seeds germinate in six to seven weeks, while old seeds take two or more years. To speed up germination on old seed, plant in pots, cover with plastic wrap, and freeze for a few days; then move to a warm place.

Uses: Cutting, border, water garden, bog.

Tufted violet; see *Viola*

Verbascum (ver-BAS-kum) **mullein** Easy ○

Zones: 6 to 8
Height: 2 to 4 feet
Colors: Amber with purple center, rose pink with maroon center, yellow with purple center
Characteristics: These old-fashioned cottage-garden plants have five-petaled flowers sometimes the size of silver dollars. They

bloom mid- to late summer on tall spikes above low rosettes of silvery gray or furry, green leaves. Plants grow quickly and could be an effective focal point in the late summer garden without needing staking. *Verbascum* has hundreds of species, most from Eurasia.

At Wave Hill, a few verbascums are allowed to seed themselves where they will. They are arresting whether planted singly or grouped architecturally. They can be planted at the front or back of the border since both the low heads of foliage and tall, open-flower stalks are handsome.

Cultural Information: Grow verbascums in average, well-drained soil, preferably alkaline (work in a little lime in spring). Remove faded flowers to encourage new basal rosettes of leaves and to help the plant live longer. New side spikes may develop. Plants are known to self-sow. Sow seeds in spring, or divide established plants in the spring. This plant sometimes behaves as a biennial.

Uses: Back of the border, accent.

Veronica (ve-RO-ni-ka) **speedwell** Moderate
○ ◑ ◣ ✳ ◣ ❀

Zones: 4 to 10 except Florida and the Gulf Coast
Height: 15 inches to 2½ feet
Colors: Blue, pink, rose, purple, white
Characteristics: Veronicas are undemanding, gracefully old-fashioned perennials, highly valued for their long season of bloom, July through September. They are widely grown for their spikes of small, closely

set flowers. The foliage is neat and often attractive. The flowers are gathered in dense, narrow spikes at the ends of the branches. The leaves sometimes have a grayish cast, are 2 inches long, lance-shaped and sit opposite one another on upright stems. The plants are long-lived and fairly restrained in growth. _Veronica spicata_, 'Minuet' has rich pink flowers in June and July, borne on 15-inch plants, and makes a fine plant for the perennial border, producing spikes that give valuable contrast in habit and texture. _V. longifolia_ var. _subsessilis_ is a 2-foot-tall, dark blue variety, that flowers in July. The cultivar 'Sunny Border Blue' is my favorite because of the intense blue of the flowers.

Cultural Information: Plant veronicas 1 to 2 feet apart in well-drained soil. They are exceptionally tolerant of heat and drought. Stake only plants that need it. They should be divided in the spring every two to three years when plants no longer bloom. Removing faded flowers will prolong their bloom season. Sow seeds outdoors in spring. Plants are very resistant to insects.

Uses: Cutting, border.

Viola cornuta (VEE-o-la kor-NEW-ta) **tufted violet, horned violet** Easy

◑ ○ ● ✳ ▮ ✿

Zones: 5 to 9
Height: 6 to 8 inches
Colors: Violet, lavender, yellow
Characteristics: This violet has smaller flowers than do most pansies, but it is more compact and a profuse bloomer. It is among the most valuable of low-growing perennial plants, having an extremely long blooming season, from spring to frost. It makes a handsome edger or bedding plant, and is attractive in rock garden settings. It usually does best where summers are cool.

'Princess Blue', an exceptional Burpee breeding triumph, lavishly produces its velvet, violet-blue, 1-inch flowers spring through midsummer, and then again in fall. (I've even had it bloom in my garden in late February.) The plants are only 6 inches high but spread to 10 inches. It's easy to grow from seed, and blooms in about seventy days when started indoors. It can also be grown as a flowering houseplant.

Cultural Information: Set plants 6 inches apart in rich, moist soil. Keep soil cool and lightly moist; the use of a mulch will help. Never allow the soil to become soggy. Remove all faded flowers and carefully cultivate around plants to remove any seedlings that might develop. Removal of spent blossoms encourages plants to bloom longer and stay in a neater, more vigorous condition. Divide after flowering time in the summer when plants appear to be producing fewer blooms and more foliage; lift, divide, and replant immediately.

Uses: Border, window boxes, edging, woodland gardens.

Wild indigo; see _Baptisia_

Woodland phlox; see _Phlox divaricata_

Wormwood; see _Artemesia_

Yarrow; see _Achillea_

Yucca (YUK-ka) **Adam's needle, Spanish bayonet, candles of the Lord** Easy

○ ◍ ✳

Zones: 5 to 9
Height: 5 to 6 feet
Colors: Creamy white
Characteristics: Yuccas have numerous creamy flowers on tall stems in late summer. These bold shrubs are used like perennials. They are usually thought of as desert or semidesert plants, but they are showy-flowered evergreens that can be decorative in northern gardens too, when grown in full sun. They are excellent in drought conditions. The deep-rooted, tough plants bloom in July and August, generally in alternate years. They make interesting companion plants, accent plants and background plants. It takes yuccas several years to mature and produce flowers. Because of their large, coarse, sword-like foliage, they are not for the small garden or for planting near play areas. There are some varieties with variegated foliage.

Yucca filamentosa 'Golden Sword' has a yellow strip down the leaves and 'Sunburst', with a creamy strip, has edges that turn pink in cold weather. Both have light-colored threads that curl off the edges of the leaves, softening their architectural shapes.

Cultural Information: Plant yuccas 3 feet apart in well-drained, light soil. They will tolerate sandy, poor soil. They adapt

Above: Veronica longifolia subsessilis.
Below: Viola cornuta 'Princess Blue'.

Below: Yucca filamentosa

well to high temperatures and tolerate both wet and dry summers. Most easily grown from plants. Propagate by separating rooted offshoots from the base of the plant, or take root cuttings in spring. After flowers fade, remove flower stalks unless you want the pods to dry for arrangements. All stalks should be cleaned up by late fall, for the sake of good housekeeping.

Uses: Companion, background, accent.

PERENNIAL VINES

Below: Akebia quinata

Bottom: Campsis radicans

The versatility and potential of vines in the landscape is limitless—to drape, to mantle, to conceal, to screen, to frame, to shade, to protect, to beautify, and to transform. They add grace and a romantic touch to every garden picture, but they are not grown as often as they should be. There seems to be a mystery about them that prevents many gardeners from using them. The most familiar of the vines is ivy, which clothes many a home. Notice how naked the houses look in the winter when the ivy is gone, and then look around you at all the other places a vine could enliven and enrich the landscape, a fence, shed, garage, trellis, tennis court wall, column, streetlight, bank, or tree stump. Vertical gardening adds dimension, color, fragrance, and beauty to a small space. Some vines add brilliant color to your landscape, and all contribute to the "finished look" of your gardens. Vines need only a small space, 1 to 2 square feet, for their roots to grow. If you are thinking about growing a vine against a wall or any other structure that may need repair, consider the choice of vine carefully. Some vines, like clematis, can be pulled carefully away from their support and set on the ground while you repaint (or whatever);

others, like wisteria and campsis, form tree-like trunks and can't be bent.

Vines and climbers fall into three categories: those that need to be fastened to their supports, those that climb by means of twining stems or tendrils, and those that anchor themselves by means of little "suction cups" or holdfasts. We've indicated the category for each vine.

Akebia quinata (a-KEE-bee-a kwi-NAH-ta) **fiveleaf akebia**

Easy ○ ◑ ❀

Zones: 4 to 9

Height: Up to 40 feet

Color: Purple

Characteristics: A vine worthy of high praise, which grows rapidly and adapts to both sun and partial shade. With little care, you can have a lovely twining, woody vine to train on a fence or a wall, or a vine that provides good backgrounds for flower beds. Depending on the climate, this plant will be deciduous or evergreen. It is considered hardy in Zones 4 to 9. The open habit and lovely texture of this plant makes it useful for draping over arbors or for partly hiding unsightly objects. Some gardeners even like to use it as groundcover, but it is important to note that the vine is a rapid, vigorous grower and can become invasive. With only a little more care, they can be grown indoors in a cool, light place.

This vine twists from left to right as it climbs. The leaves are compound, each with five leaflets, yellowish-green underneath, bluish-green on top in summer. Fragrant, slenderstalked flowers appear with the new leaves in the spring. The female flowers, purple-brown and about 1 inch across, are clustered with (but distinct from) the male flowers—rosy purple and ½ inch across. In the fall, 2¼- to 4-inch purple-violet sausage-like pods appear.

Cultural Information: This vine does well in moderately fertile soils that are well drained. It will take slightly acid to neutral soils (pH 6.0 to 7.0). Select an area where the plant will receive good light (it doesn't have to be direct sunlight). Do not crowd the plants, but give at least 2 feet between plantings.

If you plan to train your planting as a vine, provide a sturdy trellis or poles to train and support the plants. *Akebia quinata* grows up to 40 feet in length.

It is recommended that you prune your vine severely each year to keep the plants under control. Fall and early spring are the best times for pruning.

Plants will recover quickly if cut to the ground. *A. quinata* tolerates wind and is remarkably resistant to disease and insects.

Campsis radicans (KAMP-sis RAH-di-kanz) **trumpet vine** Native American Easy ○ ◑ ✿

Zones: 5 to 9
Height: up to 30 feet
Colors: Yellow, orange, red
Characteristics: Trumpet vine is vigorous, wonderful for midsummer color on a porch or fence when it is covered with brilliant orange-red, trumpet-shaped flowers. The compound foliage (each leaf made up of many leaflets) is dark green and trouble-free. It readily attaches itself by aerial roots, or holdfasts, that cling to walls or supports. The stems are woody, and as the vine gets older, it may become so heavy it needs the additional support of a trellis. *Campsis* can be pruned to remain bushy shrubs or hedges.
Cultural Information: This vine prefers a fertile, moderately moist soil. When transplanting a new vine it is best to cut the growth back to within a few inches of the ground, to encourage new branching and new shoots, the only ones that attach themselves to supports. Later, when your vine has reached the size you like, a yearly pruning back of the last year's growth to within 2 or 3 inches of their bases, and the removal of any dead or crowded shoots, are important. *C. radicans* can be propagated by stem cuttings, seeds or root cuttings. Grown

against a wooden building, the vine will cause problems if you want to repaint.

Clematis (KLEM-a-tis) Easy to Moderate ○ ◑ ✿

Zones: 3 to 9
Height: C. heracleifolia, 3 feet; large-flowered hybrids, 8 to 20 feet; small-flowering species up to 30 feet
Colors: Blue, white, pink, red, bicolor
Characteristics: Clematis species are among the most spectacular of flowering vines and certainly some of the most rewarding of plants. Train them on a trellis, arbor, or pergola, let them climb on a fence for a living screen, or use other plants for their supports. They can easily grow up trees, over shrubs, and among and over your climbing roses. Clematis vines can make a flowering shrub appear to be in bloom even when it's not. A forsythia that blooms in the early spring, for example, could be covered with the large purple flowers of *C. × jackmanii* from June to September. Some other popular large-flowered clematis hybrids (with flowers up to 6 inches across) are 'Ernest Markham' with ruby red blooms; 'Lincoln Star' with large, pointed flowers of delicious raspberry pink with lavender edges and dark stamens; and 'Will Goodwin', a 6- to 8-inch pure blue flower adorned with golden stamens.

The species types are smaller-flowered than the hybrids, but they grow taller, and the profusion of flowers will delight you. *C. maximowicziana* (virgin's bower), widely known as *C.*

paniculata, the sweet autumn clematis, is a favorite of mine. This vigorous vine grows to 30 feet, blooming in September and October with a profusion of 1-inch, white flowers deliciously scented like hawthorne. The flowers are followed by silvery seed heads, wonderful for winter arrangements.

C. heracleifolia is not vinelike but is rather a bushy perennial, growing to 3 feet and clothed in attractive, divided foliage. The flowers, appearing in late summer, are of rich blue, borne in clusters somewhat resembling those of hyacinths, with a delightful fragrance.
Cultural Information: Clematis vines grow best where they will receive sun at their tops and shade at their roots, the latter provided either by a ground cover or mulch. Soil should be very high in organic content, well-drained but moisture-retentive. Plant them at least 2 feet from any structure. If you'd like a vine to grow up a tree or a shrub, plant the vine several feet from the base of the tree or shrub. The vine will easily grow into and over the shrub, but for

Clematis *'Vyvan Pennell'*

Clematis *'Lincoln Star'*

Clematis × jackmanii

Lonicera heckrottii

the tree you'll need to train it up a heavy string or wire to the lower branches, and from there it can find its own way. Water during periods of drought, and fertilize and replenish the soil by mulching with compost, wood chips, pine needles, or shredded leaf mulch. Some gardeners recommend putting a flat, 12-inch stone near the vine to make sure the soil stays cool and damp on the roots. Do not incorporate chemical fertilizer into the soil; it can burn the roots. Clematis may take some time to start growth, about a month or two. They must first establish the roots in their new home. Plant about 4 feet apart.

Fiveleaf akebia; see *Akebia quinata*

Fleece vine; see *Polygonum*

Honeysuckle; see *Lonicera*

Passiflora caerulea

Lonicera (lon-i-SE-ra) **honeysuckle** Easy ○ ◐ ✸
Height: 30 feet
Zones: 5 to 9
Colors: Yellow, coral, red, white
Characteristics: Many members of the genus *Lonicera* are not vines and do not twine, but we will not discuss those here. The common honeysuckle vine tosses out long sprays of slender, tubular flowers set in pairs along the stems. The blossoms open at evening, are pure white and especially fragrant, attracting nightflying moths; after fertilization, the corollas turn pale yellow. Honeysuckle needs wire netting or a lattice to twine about, but is not otherwise fussy. It thrives at the seashore and blooms, off and on, all summer. The common yellow and white, very fragrant honeysuckle, *L. japonica* 'Halliana', runs rampant when given perfect conditions, especially in the South where it isn't checked by freezing winter. It is a better vine for northern gardens, where it is better behaved—it is not invasive, and won't climb trees, shade them from the sun, and kill them as *halliana* can. Other varieties, like *L. heckrottii*, are long-blooming with bright coral and yellow flowers. They are showier, well-behaved everywhere, and attract hummingbirds, but lack the wonderful fragrance.
Cultural Information: Honeysuckles make very few demands on the gardener. They flourish in ordinary—even poor or heavy—soils. They need to be pruned back to encourage branching or to keep them to a particular size. It is best to prune in the

fall, right after they stop flowering, or in the early spring in the North before they leaf out.

Passiflora caerulea
(pass-i-FLO-ra kie-RU-lee-a) **passion flower** Moderate ○ ◐ ✸ ✿
Zones: 5 to 9
Height: 20 feet
Colors: White with purple markings
Characteristics: Passiflora caerulea is a popular vine, easy-growing under almost any conditions. It is often used in southern and southwestern gardens, where it tolerates heat, warm to cool coastal conditions, semi-arid and arid atmospheres. Not only does it do well outdoors, but it thrives as a house- or greenhouse plant.

This vine is said to be named the "passion flower" by Spanish explorers in Brazil, because missionaries thought they saw symbols of the crucifixion in the wonderful blooms. The ten petals were thought to represent the ten apostles present at Christ's death (Peter and Judas being absent), the anthers Christ's wounds and the stigma, the nails. The delicately fringed corona resembles the crown of thorns or the halo. Finally, the five-lobed leaves represented the hands of the persecutors, and the tendrils, the whips and cords they used.

Passion flower blooms from June to September, is fragrant, and is borne solitary or in pairs. The most striking feature is the single or double row of filaments—the corona—at the base of the flower.

The edible fruit has a thick,

leathery deep purple hull (skin). About the size of plums, the fruits are said to have the combined flavor of peach, apricot, pineapple, guava, banana, lemon, and lime. Fruits are never picked from the vine but are gathered from the ground, where they fall when ripe. Fragrant, golden pulp sacs contain edible black seeds and fill the sides of the fruit.

Cultural Information: Passion flower prefers full sun, but it will tolerate partial shade and wind. A mature vine will stand 28-degree Fahrenheit temperatures. Passion flower is a rampant grower. We suggest that you do not plant it in a confined area, but rather use an outlying area of the garden. A neutral soil (pH 7.0) is best. Deep, moist, well-drained, sandy loam containing lots of good organic matter is best. Well-rotted manures may be used. Passion flower needs to be fertilized and watered properly. During periods of very hot, dry weather, you may need to apply additional water. It is most important to provide a sturdy lattice or trellis. A vigorous plant needs good supports for the tendrils to cling to. If you grow one in a pot (indoors), use bamboo stakes and attach strings against the windows so that the tendrils can take hold.

Pruning is essential to keep the passion flower growing vigorously. Prune heavily each year to thin out plants and keep them under control. Passion flower makes an excellent winter houseplant. During the early winter, it will need a rest period; grow at a temperature of 55 degrees Fahrenheit and keep it on the dry side. In late winter, increase the temperature by 15 to 20 degrees and give the plant more water. It may be necessary to repot it. Feed every two to three weeks with a mild solution of flowering houseplant fertilizer. The soil mixture should contain equal parts loam, sand, peat moss, and leaf mold. Keep soil evenly moist. The plant should be pinched back as it grows to encourage a more branched vine. The plant is almost immune to pests.

Passion flower; see *Passiflora*

Polygonum aubertii

(po-LIG-on-um o-BAIR-tee-ee) **fleece vine, silverlace vine** Easy ○ ◑ ❀

Zones: 4 to 9
Height: 20 feet
Color: White
Characteristics: This is one of the fastest growing vines, often attaining over 15 feet the first year. It is a good choice to provide screening for an unsightly view, or to cover a large expanse of fence beautifully and rapidly. It clings to any support without harming it and provides huge billowing sprays of white summer flowers.

Cultural Information: Polygonum aubertii is not particular about soil as long as it is moist but well-drained. Too rich a soil can result in excessively coarse growth. Pruning in late winter or early spring is best to contain growth and shape.

Silverlace vine; see *Polygonum*

Trumpet vine; see *Campsis*

Polygonum aubertii

A Gold Medal for Burpee

Occasionally a gold medal is awarded for a major breakthrough in breeding. This happened in 1988, when Burpee breeder Denis R. Flaschenreim, Ph.D., introduced Coreopsis 'Early Sunrise'. It won gold medals from both All-America Selections and Fleuroselect, its European counterpart, as the first perennial to consistently bloom within one hundred days from sowing. No other perennial has ever won over annuals in this regard. The first perennial coreopsis to bloom the first year from seed—in just eleven weeks from indoor sowing—it bears rich, golden yellow, semidouble blooms on uniform 24- to 26-inch plants, and it continues to bloom until heavy frost, returning year after year to produce a full summer of bloom.

PLACEMENT OF PERENNIALS IN A BORDER

Bloom times are based on Zone 7. They are approximate and cover a range of dates, so plants may not bloom for the whole time given. Keep in mind that a cool spring will delay bloom, and a warm one will speed it up. Check plant portraits in this chapter for more detailed information on individual species and length of bloom.

Front of the Border

PERENNIAL	BLOOM TIME
Artemisia (mugwort)	Foliage attractive May–October
Astilbe (garden spirea)	June–July
Aubretia (rainbow rock cress)	April–June
Aurinia (basket of gold)	April–June
Campanula (bellflower)	June–September
Cerastium (snow-in-summer)	May–June
Chrysanthemum	August–November
Dianthus (pinks)	May–June
Dicentra eximia (bleeding heart)	May–August
Gaillardia (blanket flower)	June–October
Heuchera (coralbells)	June–July
Hosta (funkia)	July–September
Iberis sempervirens (candytuft)	April–May
Liriope muscari (lilyturf)	July–August
Lysimachia (loosestrife)	July–August
Nepeta (catmint)	May–September
Oenothera (evening primrose)	May–June
Phlox divaricata (woodland phlox)	April–June
Phlox stolonifera (creeping phlox)	May–June
Phlox subulata (mountain pinks)	April–May
Primula (primrose)	April–June
Pulmonaria (lungwort)	March–April
Sedum (stonecrop)	June–September
Stachys (lamb's ears)	Foliage attractive May–October
Viola cornuta (tufted violet)	April–June, September

Middle of the Border

PERENNIAL	BLOOM TIME
Achillea (yarrow)	June–July
Amsonia (blue-star)	May–June
Anchusa azurea (Italian alkanet)	May–June
Anemone × hybrida (hybrid anemone)	September–October

PERENNIAL	BLOOM TIME
Aquilegia (columbine)	May–June
Artemisia (mugwort)	Foliage attractive May–October
Asclepias tuberosa (butterfly weed)	July–September
Aster (hardy aster)	August–September
Astilbe (garden spirea)	June–July
Baptisia australis (false indigo)	June–July
Campanula (bellflower)	June–September
Centaurea (knapweed)	June–July
Centranthus ruber (red valerian)	June–August
Chrysanthemum	September–November
Coreopsis (tickseed)	June–September
Delphinium	June–September
Dianthus (pinks)	May–June
Dicentra spectabilis (bleeding heart)	May–June
Dictamnus albus (gas plant)	June–July
Gaillardia (blanket flower)	June–October
Gypsophila paniculata (baby's breath)	June–September
Helleborus (hellebore)	February–April
Hemerocallis (daylily)	June–September
Hosta (funkia)	July–September
Iris (bearded iris)	May–June
Kniphofia uvaria (red-hot poker)	August–September
Liatris (gayfeather)	July–August
Lobelia (cardinal flower)	August–September
Lunaria (silver-dollar plant)	May–June
Lupinus (lupine)	June
Lychnis (champion)	June–August
Lysimachia (loosestrife)	July–August
Malva sylvestris (mallow)	July–August
Nepeta (catmint)	May–September
Oenothera (evening primrose)	May–June
Paeonia (peony)	May–June
Papaver orientale (Oriental poppy)	June
Phlox paniculata (garden phlox)	July–September
Physalis alkekengii (Chinese lantern)	August–September
Physostegia (obedient plant)	July–October

PERENNIAL	BLOOM TIME
Platycodon (balloon flower)	June–October
Rudbeckia (black-eyed Susan)	July–September
Salvia (meadow sage)	June–September
Saponaria officinalis (double bouncing bet)	June–July
Scabiosa caucasica (pincushion flower)	June–August
Sedum (stonecrop)	June–September
Stokesia (Stoke's aster)	June–July
Trollius (globeflower)	June–July
Verbascum (mullein)	July–August
Veronica (speedwell)	June–August

Back of the Border

PERENNIAL	BLOOM TIME
Acanthus mollis (bear's britches)	June
Alcea rosea (hollyhock)	July–August
Anchusa azurea (Italian alkanet)	May–June
Aster (hardy aster)	August–September
Baptisia australis (false indigo)	June–July
Boltonia asteroides	July–October
Cimicifuga racemosa (bugbane)	July–August
Delphinium ('Giant Pacific')	June–July, September
Echinacea (coneflower)	July–September
Echinops (globe thistle)	July–August
Hemerocallis (daylily)	June–September
Kniphofia uvaria (red-hot poker)	August–September
Liatris (gayfeather)	July–August
Lythrum salicaria (purple loosestrife)	June–September
Monarda (bee balm)	July–August
Perovskia atriplicifolia (Russian sage)	August–September
Phlox paniculata (garden phlox)	July–September
Rudbeckia (black-eyed Susan)	July–September
Verbascum (mullein)	July–August
Yucca (Adam's needle)	July

See page 15 for further information on designing your garden.

PESTS AND DISEASES

Perennials are one of the easiest groups of plants to grow successfully. When properly planted in well-prepared soil to their liking, they shouldn't be bothered by many pests or diseases. Of course, a healthy plant is better able to ward off attacks. If you are alert, checking your plants (especially the undersides of leaves) regularly for pests, you will be able to detect any problems early when they are easier to eliminate.

Your plants will give you clear signs about how they feel. Wilted, droopy leaves may simply indicate a lack of water (always the first thing to check) or too much water. Is your plant drowning from poor drainage and not enough air? Check the soil to see if it is soggy; if so, you need to dig the plant up and improve the drainage. A third possibility is an insect or disease problem. Check the leaves, tops and bottoms, to see if something is eating them. Check the stems for bruises or holes where borers or tunnelling insects might have burrowed and cut off the plant's source of nutrients.

Act quickly when you find a problem. At Burpee we believe in natural controls that won't harm the environment. Over the years we have watched chemicals come and go, first introduced as miracle controls for pests or diseases, then branded as endangering the environment. There are many safe, organic controls on the market. We particularly recommend Safer™ insecticidal soaps, and Ringers® natural pest controls. Many insect problems can be effectively treated with an insecticidal soap.

Rules for a Healthy Garden

1. Mother Nature varies the plants in her gardens for a good reason. Different plants are susceptible to different diseases, and a disease is more easily contained when there is a variety of plants in the same garden. If all of your plants are the same variety, it is more likely that a disease that infects one will spread.

2. A perennial that is not doing well in one part of your garden deserves a chance in another part; then, if it is a persistent troublemaker, get rid of it. Be tough. Make your plants perform, or grow something else. There are so many wonderful perennials that will grow in your area with a minimum of problems that if you spent a lifetime pursuing them all, you'd still be left with new and untried varieties.

3. Remember that every gardening year is different, and even the same perennial plants look different from year to year. Seasonal pest problems also vary from year to year, as does the severity of any disease. If you keep a notebook of the problems you encounter over the course of a year, it will help you prepare for and, hopefully prevent, them the next year.

4. Don't water at night. Wet soil invites slugs to an orgy.

5. Keep your garden clean. Don't leave dead flowers, leaves, or other garden refuse near the plants, because they provide perfect hiding places and homes for insects and slugs. Fall cleanup is especially important. As perennials die back to the ground, their decaying foliage can be a winter housing and breeding place for pests and disease. This foliage, on the other hand, makes a great addition to the compost heap.

6. Not all insects are bad. Learn to distinguish between the harmful and the helpful. Ladybugs, praying mantis, green lacewings, and tricogramma wasps are beneficial insects. You can purchase them from Burpee's mail order gardening catalogs and release them in your garden for help in keeping pests in line.

Many kinds of insects and diseases trouble perennials, but not all are found in all parts of the country, and a perennial gardener is rarely bothered by many at the same time. Remember, you'll probably never have a perfect garden every year, because wind, rain, hot sun, insects, and disease can all do damage, but you can have a beautiful garden most of the time. Hard work, patience, and planning all pay big dividends in gardens. Some of the problems you might encounter are the following:

DISEASES

Botrytis

Another name for botrytis is "gray mold blight," a pretty good description of what to look for. Caused by humid conditions, it can be controlled by good air circulation, good sanitation, and prompt removal of any diseased part to avoid spreading. Safer's™ Garden Fungicide can be used as a preventative.

Powdery Mildew

When powdery mildew is present, the plants look like they are covered with a dirty, white dust. Not only is it unattractive, but it also causes leaves to curl and dry out, and buds to die before blooming. By giving plants good air circulation, watering only in the morning (with soaker hoses, not overhead sprinklers), problems can be kept to a minimum. However, some plants are extremely susceptible, like garden phlox. Safer's™ Garden Fungicide is a good preventative that doesn't leave a noticeable residue. Look for perennial varieties that are disease-resistant, of course.

INSECTS

Spider Mites

If you discover tiny red spots on the underside of leaves, your plant doesn't have the measles. It's an attack of spider mites. They pierce the leaves and suck out the plant's juices, causing the leaves to yellow, wither, and drop off. Wash affected plants with a strong spray of cold water or spray with an organic insecticide to help to control them. Ladybugs are the spider mites' natural enemy.

Aphids

Their method of damaging plants is similar to that of spider mites but, in addition, when they suck out the plant's juices, they can introduce infections and spread disease from one plant to another. Aphids are soft-bodied, pear-shaped and multicolored. Although they are quite small, they're usually not difficult to see since they arrive in mobs. A strong spray of water or an organic insecticide will help to dispel and destroy them.

Beetles

A variety of beetles attacks perennials, but the Japanese beetle is the most in evidence. Use beetle traps that work by luring male beetles with a powerful sex attractant and female beetles with a floral attractant. Beetles should also be treated while in their grub stage, living in the soil, and feeding on the roots of grass. Ringer's® Grub Attack kills by infecting grubs with Milky Spore, a disease caused

by *bacillus popilliae*, a natural ingredient. The grubs stop feeding and die, releasing billions of new spores to kill other grubs. A single application continues to work for ten or more years.

Leafhoppers

These wedge-shaped insects are small and green, gray, or yellow in color. They carry and spread disease as they suck juices from plants. Plant growth is stunted, buds do not blossom, and the leaves yellow. Ladybugs, green lacewings, and praying mantises love leafhoppers for dinner. Use an insecticidal soap early in the day when the insects are less active.

Whiteflies

Another sucking insect, only 1/16 inch in size but with extra-large white wings. They travel in groups and therefore are very easy to see. If you disturb a leaf on which they are feeding, a cloud of what appears to be white dust will rise. Pest strips coated with a sticky substance and colored yellow—a favorite with whiteflies—attract them like magnets and make it easy to control them. These strips are non-poisonous, odorless, and readily available at garden centers.

Japanese Beetles

Along with all of the wonderful imports from the Orient have come some less welcome ones. The Japanese beetle sneaked ashore in August of 1916 in New Jersey, hidden in the soil of nursery stock. The beetles were quickly detected in a 2½-square-mile area, and plans were made to eradicate them. A barrier around the affected area ½- to 1-mile wide was to be cut, burned, and sprayed. Unfortunately, the plans were not carried out until a year later, and even though it is estimated that 1.5 million beetles were killed,

enough had escaped to infect 48 square miles during that year.

Today, Japanese beetles are the bane of gardeners east of the Mississippi, and the beetles continue to spread west. They'll eat almost anything: leaves, flowers, grass, and fruit. They live for 30 to 40 days, laying their eggs to hatch in the soil, where the larvae proceed to live and eat the roots of grass for about four months. The larvae hibernate for the winter and emerge as adult beetles in the summer, to continue the cycle.

SLUGS AND SNAILS

If they were entered side by side in a beauty contest, the snails would win because their slimy, wormlike bodies are hidden by shells. Slugs and snails act alike, coming out at night or after a rain to devour foliage. They live in mulch and garden waste. The brave can pick them off and squash or step on them. The rest of us simply need to spread diatomaceous earth (ground, fossilized aquatic plants, available in bags from garden supply stores) around the base of plants. Slugs and snails hate crawling through rough soil, and they find diatomaceous earth too scratchy for their smooth skin. Another

effective, time-honored method of control is to sink a bowl of beer into the garden, leaving the rim at soil level; attracted by the beer, the slugs will crawl into the bowl and drown.

GARDENERS' MOST-ASKED QUESTIONS

The first Burpee catalog was mailed in 1876, and the catalogs have been coming ever since, offering gardeners a wealth of seeds, plants, fruits, shrubs, and trees, as well as advice for better gardening. From the earliest years, Burpee has received letters from customers describing their gardens and asking questions. Today our "Gardening Hot Line" receives over thirty-five thousand phone calls a year. Here are the most frequently asked questions about perennials.

PLANNING

Q: I have a very small garden, and would like to have flowers always in bloom. Can I plant my perennials closer together to fill my garden better?

A: Don't plant more closely together than recommended. Crowded plants don't perform well and are more susceptible to disease. Layering in the garden is an effective way to enjoy flowers all season long. Spring-, summer- and fall-blooming bulbs can be planted under various perennials to grow up through their foliage, adding flowers to the garden when the perennial blooms may themselves be less than triumphant. Lily and daffodil bulbs, for example, are each about the size of a baseball and should be planted 8 inches deep. They have small roots that take up little room and don't interfere with the large roots of other perennials. The early spring bulbs *Eranthis*, snowdrops, and scilla are small—the size of a thimble—and take up even less room, adding bloom to the garden when very few perennial flowers bloom. Shallow-rooted annuals such as *Alyssum* can be grown between perennials and won't grow deep enough to interfere with their perennial neighbors.

Q: Which perennials bloom all summer?

A: Few perennials bloom all summer, but many have long bloom seasons. They include *Coreopsis* species, *Hemerocallis* 'Stella De Oro', *Platycodon* species, and *Aster × frikartii*, all of which will bloom for three months or longer if dead flower heads are removed before going to seed. For the length of bloom of your favorite flowers, check the "Plant Portraits" (page 35).

Q: Can perennials be combined with annuals?

A: Yes, very well! Annuals can be very useful in perennial beds, especially while you are waiting for the perennials fill in. Annuals can provide color all season long in areas of your perennial beds.

Q: We have a wet area on our property that rarely dries out. Can I plant perennials there?

A: There are many perennials that like to have their feet wet. Among them are: the cardinal flower (*Lobelia cardinalis*), loosestrife (*Lythrum virgatum* 'Morden's Pink'), Japanese iris (*I. kaempferi*), bee balm (*Monarda* species), marsh marigold (*Caltha* species), forget-me-not (*Myosotis* species), Siberian iris (*I. sibirica*), astilbe, and globe flower (*Trollius* species). For a more complete list, check the "Plant Portraits" (page 35).

Q: Which perennials thrive in shade?

A: Try hostas, columbines, astilbes, coralbells, hellebores, bergenias, dicentras, Japanese anemones, tiarellas, primulas, pulmonarias, and cimicifugas, to name a few. Refer to the "Plant Portraits" (page 35) for information on how your favorite perennials fare in shade. Groundcovers and perennials with variegated foliage brighten a shady spot all season even when absent of blooms.

Q: What flowers do you recommend for fall and winter bloom for Zones 8, 9, and 10?

A: Dianthuses, chrysanthemums, gerberas, gladioluses, gloriosa lilies, gypsophilas, hollyhocks, iberis, and lobelias, are just a few of the many possibilities.

These ladies were busy answering the many inquiries received by the W. Atlee Burpee Company at the turn of the century.

Q: *Which perennials can I grow in Florida? Can I grow peonies there?*
A: Peonies need a cold winter 'sleep' and are not suited to Florida's climate. However, many perennials thrive in a Florida climate: yarrows (*Achillea* species), alyssums, baby's breath (*Gypsophila* species), snow-in-summer (*Cerastium* species), balloon flowers (*Platycodon* species), columbines (*Aquilegia* species), coreopsis, pinks (*Dianthus* species), bee balm (*Monarda* species), Oriental poppies (*Papaver orientale*), Shasta daisies (*Chrysanthemum maximum*), and sweet peas (*Lathyrus latifolius*).

Q: *What perennials can be grown in Zones 2 and 3?*
A: It is important to remember that perennials in these cold areas should be transplanted in the spring, not the fall. This will ensure proper establishment of the root system. Provided the plants are thoroughly established in the soil, these need no special protection: aquilegias, asters, campanulas, centaureas, coreopsis, day-lilies, delphiniums, hostas, lilies of the valley, peonies, phloxes, and rudbeckias.

The following would benefit by some winter protection against freezing and thawing conditions (salt hay, pine boughs, and the like—see page 33): achilleas, aconites, chrysanthemums, dianthuses, and ferns.

PLANTING

Q: *I had poor germination with my seeds this year. What did I do wrong?*
A: Many factors contribute to poor germination. The most common are:

1. Sowing too early in the season. Some varieties require warm, dry soils.
2. Planting too deeply. Petunias, impatiens, snapdragons, and begonias, to name a few, require light to sprout.
3. Damping off. A fungus present in most soils can kill seeds or seedlings at or below the soil line. Give proper ventilation, light, and heat where necessary.
4. Forgetting to water, especially with perennial or biennial seeds. Drying out of the seedbed or container for just an hour or so can mean disaster.
5. Outdoor sowing may be washed away in spring rains, and sometimes seed is eaten by birds.

Q: *How do I plant my bare-root peony?*
A: Locate the eyes on the root, on the top. Plant so the eyes are 1 to 2 inches below the soil level in a rich, well-drained soil. Peonies are long-lived plants, but they may not flower for one or two years. It's worth the wait!

Q: *How do I plant my bare-root hosta or daylily?*
A: Dig a hole wider than a circle whose radius is the length of the roots, and about 3 to 4 inches deep. Make a little mound on the bottom of the hole. Spread the roots out over the mound with the crown (the place where the roots meet the top growth) on top and fill the hole so about 1 inch of soil is on top of the crown.

Q: *My perennials just arrived and they look brown and damaged or dead. What's wrong?*
A: Your plants are in a dormant condition. They have begun their natural process of 'sleeping' for the winter. Give them a chance and we are sure you will be happy in the spring.

Q: *Is it too late to plant or transplant in October?*
A: You can plant as late as October in most parts of the country, with the notable exceptions of Zones 3, 4, and possibly 5 (if there has been hard frost). Perennials can be moved as long as the soil is not frozen too hard to dig. The only danger is that in extremes of freezing and thawing, the roots might be pushed up out of the ground. After the first heavy frost, mulch to keep the soil warm and prevent this from happening. It is best to transplant on a cool, cloudy day or late in the day to lessen transplant shock. For more information on transplanting, turn to page 30.

Q: *We had an unusually early snow and my plants just arrived. Is it really all right to plant now when it is snowing?*
A: Snow itself is not a problem. The problem is whether the ground has frozen too hard to dig and if the soil has been properly prepared. Since mail-order plants are shipped in the fall, not in the winter, you are probably experiencing an early snow. The weather should clear in a few days and then your plants can be safely planted in the garden. Until then, the plants will keep well in a cool place—50 degrees Fahrenheit is perfect—with indirect light and adequate water.

GROWING

Q: When do I know it's time to divide my perennials?

A: Some perennials need to be divided every three years, some every four or five years, and some never need dividing at all. When you see the growth looking crowded or overgrown and bloom seems to be affected, it's time to divide. Check the "Plant Portraits" (page 35) for specific information on individual plants.

Q: What is the best time of year to divide and/or transplant my perennials?

A: Divide in the fall or spring and transplant at the same time. To divide, dig up the plants and literally cut the clump in half with a spade or a knife. Be brutal! Plant the extra plant in another part of your garden or give it to a friend.

Q: When should I cut my perennials back, fall or spring?

A: Some perennials, such as astilbes and *Sedum* 'Autumn Joy', have a very decorative winter form. Generally, however, it is a good idea to cut back dead foliage in fall, adding it to your compost pile. This prevents pest and disease organisms from finding a winter home in these plant parts. If you don't have time in fall, cut back in early spring.

Q: I've raked all the leaves from my lawn and flower border, so as not to smother the grass or plants. Was this the right thing to do?

A: Leaves should be raked off the lawn because they will smother the grass. However, they may be left in the flower border as a mulch, unless the accumulation of leaves is deep enough to prevent water from penetrating the soil. Whole leaves give the garden a messy look, whereas shredded leaves blend with the soil and don't distract from the garden. The best procedure is to either shred the leaves and return them to the garden, or put them in a compost pile (see page 25), returning them to the garden after they have decomposed. Put any excess leaves in the compost pile. Composting and mulching with organic materials is the most important organic way to feed and improve the soil.

Q: Why are my chrysanthemums turning brown?

A: The flowers turn brown when the season is over. Cut the plant back to 4 to 6 inches above ground. This prevents winter winds from damaging the plants by breaking off fragile, dying stalks. Insects and disease can more easily enter bruised or open stems. If the plants are infected with insects, cut them back to ground level and burn or thoroughly dispose of the infected stalks.

Blooms that brown before opening may be troubled by nematodes, insects that can't be seen without a magnifying glass. If you suspect nematodes are the problem, transplant your chrysanthemums into a new area and watch them closely until they become established (this should take a few weeks). Remember that chrysanthemums need dividing every spring. This is a good time to examine the roots for any signs of rot or disease, which can easily be cut out from the roots. Severely rotted roots indicate the plant should be discarded.

Q: How do I control iris borers?

A: This is the most serious problem for irises. Holes made by the borers make irises susceptible to disease and bacterial soft rot which can quickly soften and destroy the rhizomes (the equivalent of a root for iris). In the fall, the borer moth lays its larvae on the old, browning iris leaves. The larvae are protected from winter weather in the dead foliage; in the spring they eat their way through the stem and down into the rhizomes. To prevent this, remove all flower stalks, leaves, and other debris in the fall. This will eliminate any borer eggs deposited on the lower portions of the plants. In the spring, examine the new leaves closely.

As a precaution, you can spray with a mild insecticide soap solution. Crush any larvae found in the leaves. If the problem persists and your iris become diseased, plant in a different area of the garden with well-drained, well-prepared soil; provide adequate spacing for plants and plenty of sun. Avoid overwatering and the use of wet mulches, which can encourage borers and disease.

Q: How do I protect my plants for winter?

A: After the ground freezes, cover it with pine boughs, salt hay, or 3 to 4 inches of shredded fall leaves to help prevent frost-heaving. In areas where there are at least 5 or 6 inches of snow and gardeners won't see the ground again until spring, small perennial plants should be potted up in containers, watered well, and kept outside in a protected location.

Q: How do vines climb?

A: Vines climb by various methods. There are the "graspers" like sweet peas (*Lathyrus* species) that wrap tendrils (slender, threadlike organs) around nearby supports. Then there are "twiners" like *Clematis* species, which climb by wrapping their stems around the support as they pull themselves up, and *wisteria* species, "twiners" that climb by wrapping their stems around a nearby support. (Once established, wisteria develop trunks like those of trees, and can support themselves. Even then, their weight can damage roofs and walls.) Finally, English ivy and climbing hydrangea are "clingers," supported by aerial rootlets that hold fast like tiny suction cups to any surface—even smooth stone and masonry.

Q: It is summer now, and my spring-planted perennials are up and blooming. But they aren't nearly as full and nice as those in the picture in the catalog. What is wrong with them? They are not as tall as described.
A: Newly purchased perennials take about three years to mature to their full heights and spreads. Be patient with them and you will find your patience well rewarded.

Q: My perennials that were planted in the fall have not shown any signs of life, yet established plants are up already. Are my fall-planted plants dead?
A: No. Fall-planted perennials take longer to emerge or break dormancy in spring the first year because they must first establish a vigorous root system. In addition, some plants such as *Platycodon* break through the ground very late in spring, and care must be taken to note where they were planted so as not to disturb them. Be patient.

Please write or call for a free Burpee catalog:

W. Atlee Burpee &
  Company
300 Park Avenue
Warminster, PA 18974

215–674–9633

THE USDA PLANT HARDINESS MAP OF THE UNITED STATES

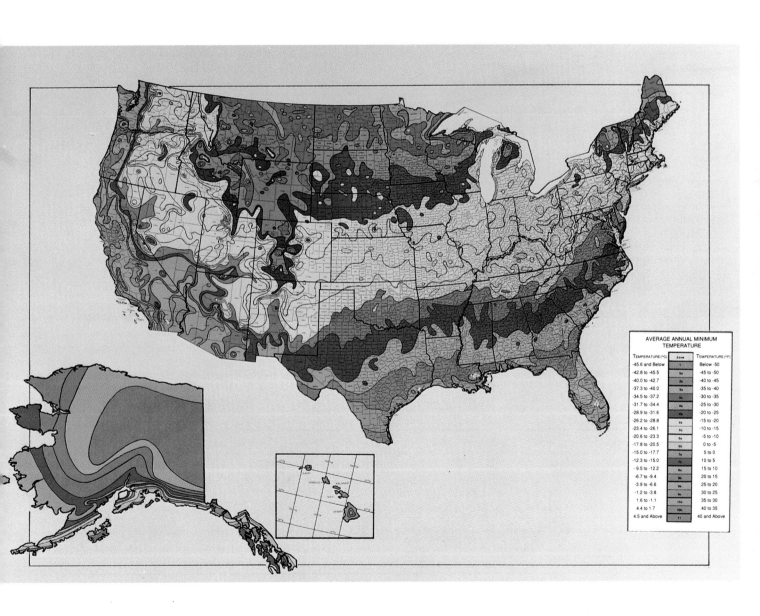

PERENNIALS CHARACTERISTICS CHART

Name	Sun/ Shade	Bloom Time	Color Range*	Space Plants	Average Height‡	Hardiness Zones†	Notes on Planting, Care, and Use
Acanthus	● ○	June	L	3–4′	3–4′	8–10	Landscape plant, back of border; likes well-drained soil, spreads rapidly
Achillea (Yarrow)	○	June–July	W, Y, R	2½–3′	1½–2′	3–8	Borders, cut flowers, dried arrangements, stands heat and drought, spreads fast, needs frequent division.
Aconitum napellus	○ ◑	August–September	B	18″	3–5′	5–9	Showy flowers ideal for the back of the border and woodland walks; likes rich, moist soil.
Alcea rosea (Hollyhock)	○	July–August	W, Y, P, R, Ro	18″	6′	3–8	Back of border, against a wall, as a screen, needs rich deep soil, staking if exposed to wind.
Amsonia tabernaemontana	○ ◑	May–June	B	12–15″	2–3′	3–8	A carefree selection for border; rarely needs division; likes moist, fertile soil.
Anchusa azurea (Alkanet)	◑ ○	May–June	Pu, B	1½′	2½–5′	3–8	Border, cutting, naturalizing open spaces, needs well-drained soil.
Anemone x hybrida (Japanese Anemone)	● ◑ ○	September–October	W, Ro	18″	2–3½′	5–8	Borders, informal plantings, spreads rapidly, needs moisture-retentive soil.
Aquilegia (Columbine)	◑ ○	May–June	B, P, R, Y	2′	1½′–3′	4–8	Borders, cutting, rock gardens, informal woodland settings, needs well-drained, moisture-retentive soil.
Artemisia	○	—	—	12–18″	6–8″	5–8	Borders, rock gardens, cutting, silver foliage, needs sandy well-drained soil.
Asclepias tuberosa (Butterfly Weed)	○	July–September	O	12–18″	2–3′	4–9	Cutting, dried wild flowers, middle of border. Highly heat- and drought-tolerant. Attracts butterflies. Once established, taproot makes difficult to transplant.
Aster	○ ◑	August–September	W, B, O, Y	2′	18″–5′	3–8	Borders, cutting, easy to grow, pinch back in spring for good branching.
Astilbe	◑ ○	June–July	W, P, R	1′	1–3½′	4–8	Borders, cutting, woodland setting with ferns and hosta, needs rich, moist soil.

‡Turn to plant portraits for heights of specific species.
*Color range abbreviations are the following: B—Blue; L—Lavender; Pu—Purple; P—Pink; Ro—Rose; Br—Brown; R—Red; O— Orange; Y—Yellow; W—White.
†See The USDA Plant Hardiness Map of the United States, page 85.

Name	Sun/ Shade	Bloom Time	Color Range*	Space Plants	Average Height‡	Hardiness Zones†	Notes on Planting, Care, and Use
Aubrieta deltoidea	○ ◐	April–June	P, Ro, Pu	12″	6″	4–7	Excellent for rock gardens and groundcover; combine with spring bulbs; likes rich well-drained soil.
Aurinia saxatilis	○	April–June	Y	1–2′	6–12″	4–8	Good for rock gardens; combine with spring bulbs; tolerates poor or sandy soil.
Baptisia australis	○ ◐	June–July	B	18–24″	3–4′	3–9	Good for the back of the border; nice with Oriental poppy; likes well-drained soil.
Boltonia asteroides 'Snowbank'	○ ◐	July–October	W	2–2½′	4–5′	4–9	Use as accent plant, cuttings. Likes well-drained soils. Silvery foliage provides excellent contrast in the back of the border.
Campanula carpatica (Carpathian Harebell)	○ ◐	June–September	B, W	10–12″	6″–4′	3–7	Fine for edging, the front of the border or in the rock garden. Use summer mulch to keep roots cool.
Centaurea dealbata	○	June–July	P	2′	2–4′	4–8	Border; not fussy about soil; blooms longer in cool weather.
Centranthus ruber	○ ◐	June–August	R	18″	2–4′	5–9	Border; likes dry soil; good cutting flower and for potpourri.
Cerastium tomentosum (Snow-in-Summer)	○	May–June	W	10–12″	4–6″	2–8	Fine for edging, groundcover or rock gardens; grown for its woolly silver foliage. Needs good drainage.
Chrysanthemum coccineum (Pyrethrum)	○ ◐	June–July	W, P, R	18″	15–30″	5–9	Excellent for cutting, corsages, and accent among shrubs.
Chrysanthemum (Garden Varieties)	○	August–November	All except Blue	15–24″	1–3′	5–9	Outstanding as a source of autumn garden color and for long-lasting cut flowers. Pinch back repeatedly until buds form to promote bushier growth. Divide every one to two years, replanting the vigorous outside growths.
Chrysanthemum maximum (Shasta Daisy)	○ ◐	June–September	W	15–18″	10–30″	5–9	A fine plant for the midborder and unsurpassed for cutting. Divide every two to three years.
Chrysanthemum pacificum	○ ◐	October–November	Y	3′	18″	5–9	Mound-shaped plants with attractive variegated foliage and bright-yellow flowers in fall. Outstanding for edging and for groundcover.

Name	Sun/ Shade	Bloom Time	Color Range*	Space Plants	Average Height‡	Hardi- ness Zones†	Notes on Planting, Care, and Use
Cimicifuga simplex (Bugbane)	◑	August– September	W	2′	3–6′	3–8	Graceful plant, topped with elegant spires of white. Fine for woodlands or shaded borders.
Coreopsis	◑ ○	June–September	Y	1–1½′	2½–3′	3–9	Carefree subjects for the mid-border, widely tolerant of soils.
Delphinium	◑ ○	June–September	W, B, P	1½–3′	1–5′	3–8	Stately plants; the taller ones magnificent in the back of the border, where they require staking. Shorter kinds used in midborder need no staking. Best where nights are cool. Cut back after June bloom.
Dianthus (Pinks)	○	May–June	W, P, R, Ro, Y	8–12″	5–12″	3–8	Fine plants for edging, the front of the border or in the rock garden.
Dicentra spectabilis (Showy Bleeding Heart)	◑	May–June	P, W	2′	1–2½′	3–9	Gracefully pendent branches bear heart-shaped flowers. Excellent in combination with late-blooming tulips. Plants die back and become dormant in summer.
Dicentra eximia 'Zestful'	◑	May–August	P	2′	18″	3–9	Attractive blue-green ferny foliage —exquisite rosy pendent flowers. Best in moist soil enriched with organic matter.
Dictamnus albus	○ ◑	June–July	P, W	3′	3′	3–8	Border; this long-lasting flower is slow growing.
Digitalis (Foxglove)	◑	June–July	P, Pu, W, R, Y	1′	3′	2–9	Excellent for back of the border. Evergreen in all but coldest climates. Stake if exposed to strong wind.
Echinacea (Coneflower)	○ ◑	July–September	Pu, W	18–24″	2–5′	3–9	For midborder and cutting. Widely adaptable and drought-resistant.
Echinops ritro	○	July–August	B	18–24″	4–5′	3–8	Back of the border; likes well-drained soil; good for cutting and drying.
Eupatorium purpureum (Joe Pye Weed)	○ ◑	August– September	P	2½–3′	4–6′	3–9	A majestic native plant with red stems—combines marvelously with taller ornamental grasses and makes a fine showing in the back of the border. Tolerant of many soils.

‡Turn to plant portraits for heights of specific species.
*Color range abbreviations are the following: B—Blue; L—Lavender; Pu—Purple; P—Pink; Ro—Rose; Br—Brown; R—Red; O— Orange; Y—Yellow; W—White.
†See The USDA Plant Hardiness Map of the United States, page 85.

NAME	SUN/ SHADE	BLOOM TIME	COLOR RANGE*	SPACE PLANTS	AVERAGE HEIGHT‡	HARDI- NESS ZONES†	NOTES ON PLANTING, CARE, AND USE
Gaillardia (Blanket Flower)	○	June–October	Y, R	12–36″	12–18″	3–9	Brilliant color in the border; excellent for cutting. Demand well-drained soil; highly drought-tolerant.
Gaura lindheimeri	○	July–August	W, P	18″	3–4′	6–9	Back of the border; likes sandy soil enriched with compost; long-blooming.
Gypsophila (Baby's Breath)	○	June–September	W	3′	3–4′	3–10	Sprays of tiny flowers, ideal border filler and perfect for cutting. Likes rich soil; tolerates lime. Taller kinds need support.
Helleborus orientalis (Lenten Rose)	◑	February–April	P, Pu, W	15″	1–3′	4–9	Late winter and early spring color. Evergreen. Superb to underplant broad-leaved evergreens.
Hemerocallis (Daylily)	○ ◑	June–September	Y, O, P, R, L	2′	18″–5′	3–10	Among the easiest of all perennials. Fine for midborder (dwarfer varieties for edging), grouped by themselves or with iris. Established plantings become so dense they are practically weed-free. Divide when overcrowded.
Heuchera (Coralbells)	○ ◑	June–July	P, W, R	1″	1–2′	4–8	Evergreen in all but the coldest areas, attractive for foliage and flowers. Mid- to front border. Enrich soil with organic matter, benefits from winter mulch.
Hosta	◑ ●	July–September	W, L	1–3′	18″–3′	3–9	Outstanding shade plant, for its foliage may be green, yellow, blue, or variegated. Many have fragrant flowers. Enjoy soil enriched with organic matter. Need virtually no maintenance.
Iberis (Candytuft)	○ ◑	April–May	W	6–12″	16″	4–8	Evergreen plants, excellent for edging and in the rock garden. Shearing back extends bloom period. Likes well-drained soil.
Iris, Bearded	○	May–June	W, P, R, O, B, Pu, L, blends	12–18″	6″–4′	4–9	Unsurpassed for late spring color. Dwarf types are fine for the front of the border or the rock garden. Intermediate types are for mid-border, tall types toward the rear or combined with daylilies. Plant with rhizome top even with soil surface; need good drainage. Divide every 3 to 4 years.

Name	Sun/ Shade	Bloom Time	Color Range*	Space Plants	Average Height‡	Hardi-ness Zones†	Notes on Planting, Care, and Use
Iris sibirica	○ ◐	June	B, W	12–18″	2–3′	4–9	Prefers well-drained but moisture-retentive soils. Need no dividing.
Kniphofia (garden hybrids)	○	August–September	R, Y, OW	1½–2′	2–4′	6–9	Back of the border; likes moist, sandy loam; lovely cut flowers.
Liatris scariosa (Gayfeather)	○	July–August	W, Ro, P, Po	2′	2–6′	4–9	A fine plant for the back of the border or for the waterside. Easy to grow in almost any well-drained soil. Deadhead to encourage additional flowering.
Liriope (Lily Turf)	○ ◐ ●	July–August	L, N, Pu	10–12′	12–18″	6–10	Arching tufts of green, or variegated green and yellow foliage. Black berries in fall extend ornamental interest. Easy to grow and drought-resistant; cut back in early spring before new growth starts.
Lobelia cardinalis (Cardinal Flower)	◐ ○	August–September	R	1′	2–4′	2–8	Brilliant woodland or waterside plant; good in midborder. Likes highly organic, moisture-retentive soils.
Lunaria annula	○ ◐	May–June	W, Pu	12″	3–4′	4–8	Grown for its dried silvery seed pods, this plant prolifically self-sows; attractive spring flowers.
Lupinus (Lupine)	○ ◐	June	W, P, R, B, L, Pu, bicolors	15″	2–3′	4–7	Handsome in back or midborder. Likes cool, moisture-retentive acid soils. Deadhead to encourage additional bloom.
Lychnis coronaria (Rose Champion)	◐ ○	June–August	R, Ro, P, Pu	10–15″	1½–3′	4–8	Attractive silvery foliage, white flowers with pink eyes. Excellent in the border; foliage good groundcover.
Lysimachia clethroides	○ ◐	July–August	W, Y	18″	2½–3′	4–9	Back of the border; spreads freely.
Lythrum salicaria Morden's Pink (Purple Loosestrife)		June–September	P, Pu	2′	1½–6′	3–9	Bushy plant with numerous spikes. Mid-to-back border. Easy to grow; heat-and-drought-tolerant.
Malva moschata 'Alba' (Musk Mallow)	○	July–August	W, P	1′	2–4′	3–9	Showy hollyhock-like plant for midborder. Prefers well-drained but moisture-retentive soil. Lime if soil is very acid.
Nepeta × faassenii 'Blue Wonder' (Persian Ground Ivy)	○ ◐	May–September	B, L	1–½′	1½–2′	3–9	Silvery-green foliage, vigorous and easy to grow in almost any soil. Cutting back spent flowers often induces late reblooms.

‡Turn to plant portraits for heights of specific species.
*Color range abbreviations are the following: B—Blue; L—Lavender; Pu—Purple; P—Pink; Ro—Rose; Br—Brown; R—Red; O— Orange; Y—Yellow; W—White.
†See The USDA Plant Hardiness Map of the United States, page 85.

NAME	SUN/ SHADE	BLOOM TIME	COLOR RANGE*	SPACE PLANTS	AVERAGE HEIGHT‡	HARDI- NESS ZONES†	NOTES ON PLANTING, CARE, AND USE
Monarda (Bee Balm, Bergamot)	○ ◑	July–August	R, L, P	12–15″	2–3′	4–9	Excellent grouped in midborder or in the wild garden. Increases rapidly. Prefers moisture-retentive soil.
Oenothera speciosa (Evening Primrose)	○	May–June	P, Y, W	12–15″	10″–2′	4–8	Easy to grow, rapidly spreading plant, perfect for the border front.
Paeonia (Peony)	○ ◑	May–June	W, P, R	4′	2–4′	3–8	Outstanding for their large, often fragrant flowers and for their attractive foliage. Excellent in the midborder, in groups by themselves, or as informal hedges. Grow in sun or light shade, in well-fertilized soil. Plant with their eyes covered no more than 2 inches.
Papaver orientale (Oriental Poppy)	○	June	W, P, R	18–24″	16″–4′	3–7	Long-lived plants with large flowers, excellent in the mid-border. Plant 3 to 4 inches deep. Plants go dormant in midsummer, with new foliage appearing in fall; it is a good idea to plant a "filler" such as *Gypsophila*. Established plants resent moving.
Perovskia atriplicifolia (Russian Sage)	○	August– September	B	18–24″	2½–3′	5–9	A fine shrubby perennial for the back of the border or used as a specimen. Valued for its silvery foliage and blue flower heads, it is equally valuable in the garden and for cutting. Grow in well-drained soil.
Phlox divaricata	◑	April–June	W, L	1′	8–12″	3–8	A fine low-growing plant, excellent to carpet woodland settings and combined with daffodils. Will establish nice colonies.
Phlox paniculata (Garden Phlox)	◑ ○	July–September	W, P, R, L	15–18″	30–36″	3–9	Excellent source of color in the summer midborder. Plant in rich, well-drained but moisture-retentive soil. Deadhead to extend blooming season. Thin established plants to promote stronger growth.
Phlox stolonifera	◑	May–June	B, P	12″	6–12″	4–8	Excellent plants to naturalize in the woodland garden and for the front of the border. Given highly organic soil, will rapidly form large colonies.

Name	Sun/ Shade	Bloom Time	Color Range*	Space Plants	Average Height‡	Hardi- ness Zones†	Notes on Planting, Care, and Use
Phlox subulata (Moss or Mountain Pink)	○	April–May	P, B, R, W	8–12"	4–6'	2–9	Good for edging, as groundcover or in the rock garden. Spreads rapidly to cover banks or slopes. Easy to grow in well-drained soil.
Physalis alkekengi	○ ◐	August– September	O	1½–2'	2'	3–10	A good border flower, grown for winter bouquets; very aggressive.
Physostegia virginiana (Obedient Plant, False Dragonhead)	○ ◐	July–October	W, P	15–18"	2–3'	3–9	Clump-forming perennials, excellent for cutting and for the midborder. Plant in a moisture-retentive soil; will spread rapidly. Divide every three years.
Platycodon (Balloon Flower)	○	June–October	B, W, P	12–15"	2–3'	3–9	Easily grown perennials for the front of the border. Like well-drained soil. Late to break dormancy in the spring—do not dig them up accidentally before they sprout!
Primula (Primrose)	◐ ●	April–June	Y, P, R, B, W	6–12"	½–2'	4–7	Brightly flowered plants excellent for edging shaded beds, planting under evergreens or in groups in the woodland garden. Best grown in a moisture-retentive soil, enriched with organic matter. A winter mulch is beneficial in colder climates.
Pulmonaria (Lungwort)	● ◐	March–April	B, P, W	1'	1'	3–8	Pink buds open to blue flowers on plants ideal as groundcovers or for naturalizing. Prefers soil high in organic content.
Rudbeckia (Coneflower, Black-Eyed Susan)	○	July–September	Y, O, R	2'	2½–4'	3–9	Easy-to-grow plants for the midborder. Excellent for cutting. Widely tolerant as to soil, as long as drainage is good.
Salvia superba (Meadow Sage)	○	June–September	B	18"	18"	4–9	A fine source of concentrated, intense violet-blue color in the middle or toward the front of the border. Easy to grow in any good garden soil.
Saponaria officinalis (Bouncing Bet)	○	June–July	P	1'	2½'	3–9	Very fragrant. Forms large colonies rapidly. Mid to back of border. Thrives in almost any soil.
Scabiosa caucasica	○	June–August	B, W	10"–15"	2-½'	2–9	Good border flower with large, dense foliage; good for cutting.

‡Turn to plant portraits for heights of specific species.
*Color range abbreviations are the following: B—Blue; L—Lavender; Pu—Purple; P—Pink; Ro—Rose; Br—Brown; R—Red; O— Orange; Y—Yellow; W—White.
†See The USDA Plant Hardiness Map of the United States, page 85.

Name	Sun/ Shade	Bloom Time	Color Range*	Space Plants	Average Height‡	Hardi- ness Zones†	Notes on Planting, Care, and Use
Sedum (Stonecrop)	○ ◑	June–September	P, R, Y, W	6–18″	3–24″	3–9	Succulent plants with attractive foliage as well as appealing flowers. The lower growing sorts are at home in the rock garden or used as edging; the taller ones are fine for the midborder and effective in containers. Tolerant of almost all soils.
Stachys byzantina (Lamb's Ear)	○ ◑	Foliage attractive May–October	—	1′	1–½′	4–9	A nonflowering plant, attractive for its silvery foliage. Plant toward the front of the border. Easily grown in any well-drained soil.
Stokesia laevis	○	June–July	B, Pu, W	12″–15″	1–1½′	5–9	Border; likes well-drained soil; good cutting flower.
Trollius ledebourii (Globeflower)	○ ◑	June–July	O, Y	18″	2–3′	3–8	One of the few plants that will thrive even in poorly drained soils. Excellent cut flower.
Verbascum chaixii	○	July–August	Pu, R, Y	2′	2–4′	6–8	Back of the border; these very striking plants self-sow.
Veronica (Speedwell)	◑ ○	June–August	B, P, W, P	1–2′	15″–2½′	4–10	Free-flowering plants, fine toward the front of the border and for cutting. Exceptionally tolerant of heat and drought; plant in a well-drained soil.
Viola cornuta 'Princess Blue' (Tufted or Horned Violet)	◑	April–June, September	B, Y	6″	6″	5–9	Long-blooming plants ideal for edging woodland plantings and for the front of partially shaded beds. Best grown in moisture-retentive soils; deadheading extends the blooming period.
Yucca filamentosa	○	July	W	3′	5–6′	5–9	Good back-of-the-border or accent plants; tolerate drought and poor or sandy soil.

VINES

Name	Sun/ Shade	Bloom Time	Color Range*	Space Plants	Average Height‡	Hardi- ness Zones†	Notes on Planting, Care, and Use
Akebia quinata (Fiveleaf Akebia)	○ ◑	May	Pu	2′	40′	4–9	Divided leaved plants, ideal for trellis, wall or to grow up a tree. Large purple fruits in late summer. A vigorous grower, semi-evergreen in warmer areas. Widely adaptable to soils.

Name	Sun/ Shade	Bloom Time	Color Range*	Space Plants	Average Height‡	Hardi- ness Zones†	Notes on Planting, Care, and Use
Campsis (Trumpet Vine, Bignonia)	○ ◐	July–August	O/R, O, Y	3–6'	30'	5–9	Vigorous vines climbing by holdfasts. Trouble-free; readily attaches itself to brick, stone, or wood.
Clematis	○ ◐	June–October	P, R, L, Pu, B, W	4'	3–30'	3–9	Perhaps the most spectacular of all climbing vines. Needs support. Excellent on walls, fences, or allowed to climb on trees or climbing roses. Prefers sun at the tops, a cool, partially shaded root run. Soil should be rich and moisture-retentive, high in organic content. Water during periods of drought; fertilize with balanced plant food of several times during the growing season. In coldest areas, may die back to the roots each winter. Can be slow to start top growth; needs first to establish root system.
Lonicera × heckrottii	○ ◐	June–September	Y, R	4'	30'	5–9	These fragrant, long-blooming vines climb by twining; likes ordinary soils.
Passiflora caerulea	◐ ○	June–September	W	4'	20'	5–9	A vigorous vine, evergreen in warm climates, that climbs by tendrils.
Polygonum aubertii	○ ◐	July–August	W	4'	20'	4–9	This fast-growing vine can reach 15' the first year; clings to supports; use as a quick-growing screen.

‡Turn to plant portraits for heights of specific species.
*Color range abbreviations are the following: B—Blue; L—Lavender; Pu—Purple; P—Pink; Ro—Rose; Br—Brown; R—Red; O— Orange; Y—Yellow; W—White.
†See The USDA Plant Hardiness Map of the United States, page 85.

Index

(NOTE: Italicized page numbers refer to captions; boldface page numbers refer to the Perennials Characteristics Chart.)